Hermann Benne = Maria A. Potts
1820–1893 1818–1878

George W. Norris = Sarah A. Wagner
1833–1904 1834–1913

Henry Benne = Bertha Alvene Gravelle
1848–1923 1865–1946

David William Norris = Marie Isabel Benne
1858–1946 1891–1986

les O. iffeth -1988 = Frances R. Norris 1918–

riscilla
Griffeth

Charles
Griffeth Jr.

William C.
Griffeth

The Stranger in My Genes

a memoir

The Stranger in My Genes

a memoir

BILL GRIFFETH

Distributed by UPNE Book Partners
Hanover and London

Some of the names in this book have been changed to protect the privacy of certain individuals.

Distributed by UPNE Book Partners
1 Court Street
Lebanon, New Hampshire 03766

ISBN-13: 978-0-88082-344-9
Library of Congress Control Number: 2016940920

Design by Ellen Maxwell.

Boston, Massachusetts
2016

Contents

Introduction

This is the story of how a simple DNA test greatly complicated my life. The results suggested that I was not who I thought I was; that—incredibly—my father might not have been my father. It started me on an unsettling journey that had me questioning my most fundamental beliefs about my family and my very identity.

The DNA test was distressing, not only for the obvious reason that it forced me to rethink so many things about my life, but also because there was an especially cruel irony in all of it. For more than ten years I have been the unofficial historian of my family. Genealogy became my passion in the summer of 2003, when a cousin introduced me to family history research. Since then I have traveled tens of thousands of miles, visiting places where my family's story began in England and the Netherlands, where my seventeenth-century ancestors were born, and retracing their descendants' east-to-west migration over the next two hundred years, from Europe to America, then through Massachusetts, New York, Ohio, Illinois, Iowa, Nebraska, and Kansas. My ancestors included Puritans, pilgrims, pioneers, and even an accused witch who was hanged during the infamous Salem witch trials of 1692–93. In 2008 I published a book telling their stories, titled *By Faith Alone: One Family's Epic Journey through 400 Years of American Protestantism.*

I then spent the next four years doing research for a second, still unpublished, book about my specific line of the Griffeth family, beginning with my eighth great-grandfather, William Griffith (the original spelling of our name), a rebellious Quaker who lived on Cape Cod in the middle 1600s. Over the next 350 years, William's restless spirit ran through generations of his descendants. Some fought during the American Revolution and in the Civil War. In 1836, my third great-grandfather, Judah Griffeth, was anointed an early elder of the Mormon church in the original Mormon Temple in Kirtland, Ohio. When church founder Joseph

Smith Jr. was murdered in Illinois in 1844, members of one part of the Griffeth family followed Smith's successor, Brigham Young, to Utah, where they embraced the early Mormon lifestyle, including polygamous marriage. The other part of the family eventually settled in Kansas. I came to know all of these people as more than just names on a page. They were as real to me as my own parents and siblings are, and their stories became my stories.

But after the DNA test came back, my research came to a dead stop. If the results were correct, it meant the family tree I had spent so many years documenting with such care was not my own. It meant I was not a Griffeth.

Why am I telling this very personal story about the troubling question of my paternity? Two reasons. First, I am a journalist. I tell stories for a living. It's what I do. And objectively speaking—if that's possible—there is no denying that this is one hell of a story. Almost for that reason alone, I couldn't *not* tell it.

But the second, more important reason is that, if I'm really honest with myself, I have to admit that writing this book helped me maintain my sanity. Almost immediately after my shocking DNA test I began to keep a journal to record the surreal events that occurred, and my thoughts as they occurred to me. Being able to see these events as part of a narrative arc that I was recording as it played out allowed me to detach myself emotionally from my own story to a certain extent. And I am convinced that being detached in that way got me through my nightmare in one piece. Keeping the journal turned out to be a therapeutic exercise that helped purge my system of the pain and anger and profound sadness that I experienced over the next two years. Essentially, this book is an expanded version of my journal. My hope is that readers who may be facing similar circumstances will find some measure of comfort or reassurance in it, and from knowing that they are not alone.

For reasons that will become clear, I have changed some names and dates and places in order to protect the privacy of certain individuals.

So here is the story that I could never in a million years have imagined that I would write, about the discovery of the stranger in my genes.

Part I

There are certain queer times and occasions in this strange mixed affair we call life when a man takes this whole universe for a vast practical joke, though the wit thereof he but dimly discerns, and more than suspects that the joke is at nobody's expense but his own.

—Herman Melville, *Moby-Dick*

CHAPTER 1

The E-mail

October 4, 2012

The day my life changed forever began as just another day. Isn't that always the way? Earthquakes and lightning bolts strike without warning. If you happen to be in the wrong place at the wrong time, nothing is ever the same again. My life wasn't altered by an act of God. Instead, it was changed by the revelation of a deep dark family secret that, like a time bomb, had been ticking my whole life, and it just happened to go off on the random day when I received the e-mail.

The date was October 4, 2012. A Thursday. I was 56 years old at the time. My wife, Cindy, and I had been happily married for thirty years, and our two children were grown. Our son, Chad, was 23 and our daughter, Carlee, was 21—both great people of whom we were very proud. I had also enjoyed a long, successful career to that point as a TV news anchor, most of it spent at the cable news channel CNBC. I had everything I could have hoped for, both personally and professionally, and I thought I had life all figured out. But it turned out I didn't have a clue.

At noon that day I was sitting at my desk in the CNBC newsroom in Englewood Cliffs, New Jersey, eating a sandwich while I looked over the news wires on my computer, completely oblivious to what was about to happen. In an hour the network's car service would take me into New York City to the New York Stock Exchange, where I co-anchor a one-hour show called *Closing Bell.* At the time, my co-anchor was Maria Bartiromo. We affectionately refer to those final minutes before the bell rings as the most important hour of the trading day. So much can happen: mergers are suddenly revealed, CEO resignations are announced, and sometimes there are rumors floating around the trading floor that cause the market to move. It is a trader's job both to anticipate and to react. My job is to explain a story's significance as it was happening. I had gotten pretty good at that over the years.

On a notepad on the desk next to my sandwich I'd made a list of things I needed to do before I headed downtown:

Print Wharton scripts
Print boarding passes
Make car reservations

That evening I would be serving as master of ceremonies for the annual Joseph Wharton Awards Dinner, which honors distinguished graduates of the Wharton School of the University of Pennsylvania. The scripts I had to print out listed the biographies of the presenters and recipients I would be introducing. I am not a Wharton alumnus—I went to a state university in California—but I had been asked to host the event years earlier and had enjoyed it very much, and they liked me so they kept asking me back. On this particular evening we would be feting some pretty famous Wharton offspring: Donald Trump's daughter Ivanka would be receiving the Young Leadership Award, Estée Lauder's son Leonard would be given the Lifetime Achievement Award, and Brian Roberts, whose father Ralph Roberts cofounded Comcast, one of the country's first cable TV systems, would be given the Leadership Award. All three were obviously members of the lucky genes club, but each had found a way to emerge from the long shadows cast by their parents and achieve his or her own success.

The boarding passes I had to print were for a flight Cindy and I were taking the next morning to North Carolina, where we would be staying with friends for the weekend, and I also still needed to make reservations for the car service to take us to the airport. I was looking forward to a fun, relaxing four-day getaway, but first I had to get through this busy Thursday.

I took a bite of my sandwich and browsed the wires.

The European Central Bank continued to wrestle with crushing debt levels . . . the presidential campaign was in full swing between President Obama, who was running for reelection, and his challenger, former Massachusetts governor Mitt Romney . . . the jobs report coming out the next morning was expected to show unemployment remaining at 8.1 percent . . . nothing out of the ordinary.

Around 12:30 I reached for my Blackberry and checked my personal e-mail. There were two new messages. One was from a golf retailer; I immediately deleted it. The other was from my cousin Doug in California. My late father, Charles, and Doug's late father, Dale, were brothers. Doug and I shared a passion for family history research, and he was always sending me new tidbits he had discovered.

In the subject line, he had written, *OK, Bill, retest results are in . . .*

Doug used DNA tests to find relatives we didn't know about. And for a year or so he had been bugging me to submit a DNA sample to a lab for testing. Since we were first cousins, our Y chromosomes, which came from our fathers, would be virtually identical. His plan was to study the differences in our genes to see what he could learn about our family's history. I didn't know the first thing about genetic testing, so I just took his word for it, and I had finally submitted a sample two months earlier, in August 2012. I had swiped the inside of my cheek with two large cotton swabs the DNA-testing lab had sent and mailed them back. After that I left it to Doug to handle. A month later, in September, he told me that the lab had gotten a weird result so he'd asked them to test the sample again. Fine, I thought. Whatever.

And so now on this Thursday, October 4, the results of the retest were in. I opened his e-mail.

"Deep breath, now . . . , he wrote. *Retesting has confirmed that your paternal haplogroup is I1, not the expected R1. Your father was not Uncle Charles.*

My body responded before my brain could. I experienced a strange sensation of floating, and I could no longer feel the chair I was sitting in or the Blackberry I was holding. My breathing became labored and shallow and I heard a roaring in my ears like ocean waves crashing off in the distance. Time stopped. It was as if a movie director had yelled, "Cut!" But life in the newsroom continued all around me. Phones kept ringing, my colleagues kept talking and laughing, and the dozens of television monitors surrounding the room flickered in unison. But I was no longer a part of it. I might as well have been a thousand miles away. I felt a deep and profound aloneness.

I read the e-mail again. I had no idea what Doug was talking about. This was a story I could not explain. What were these "haplogroups" he referred to? I was an I1, he said, but I was supposed to be an R1. What did that mean? It was all just a bunch of scientific gobbledygook.

His last sentence, though, came through loud and clear:

Your father was not Uncle Charles.

This was Doug's conclusion? Just like that? How could he so hastily reach such a troubling and scandalous and life-altering judgment? Impossible! I thought. There had to be another explanation. Maybe the lab got my sample mixed up with someone else's. When I sent mine in, the DNA testing service was running a special offer. That was how Doug had enticed me to submit my sample when I did. DNA testing is not cheap. So I could imagine that the lab had been flooded with Q-tips all at once, which would have increased the chances of a mix-up. That had to be it.

Looking back, I am struck by the absurdity of that moment. There I was, sitting at my desk eating a turkey on whole wheat, and out of the blue I received an e-mail—*an e-mail!*—telling me that my father wasn't my father. (He couldn't call me?)

I fired off a reply to my cousin:

You will understand my great skepticism on all of this. I'm going to have to get a second opinion through another DNA testing service before I draw any definitive conclusions.

He responded immediately:

Good call. Shall I compile a list of other companies who do paternal testing? Happy to do so.

I had to talk to somebody. I picked up the phone and called Cindy. She had long been the steadying influence in my life. I took my emotional cues from her, and I badly needed to hear her voice.

"Hey." She sounded upbeat and busy and distracted when she answered, probably packing for our trip. "What's up?"

I told her.

"That's crazy!" she shouted. Now I had her full attention. Her words were forceful, almost combative, and I thought, *This is how I should have responded.*

"But what if it's true?" I asked.

"There is no way," she said. "You're going to tell me that your mother had an affair? Think about what you're saying." She had no doubts. I exhaled. Of course there had to be a mistake. We would straighten it all out. We hung up.

Now what do I do? I could tell my producers that a family emergency had suddenly come up and leave, but where would I go? And what would I do when I got there? My day was already in motion. I had a show to do in two hours, the Wharton folks were counting on me that evening, and Cindy and I had a plane to catch the next morning. I didn't have time to dwell on this. I finished the items on my to-do list and headed outside, where my car was waiting.

The trip from CNBC's headquarters in Englewood Cliffs to the stock exchange takes roughly forty-five minutes when traffic is light. I typically use the time in the car to go over research material for the day's show. But not that day.

Ordinarily when I get in the car I chat with my driver for a few minutes about the weather or local sports teams, and then he leaves me alone to do my homework. But on this day I wasn't in the mood for small talk. No words were spoken. We crossed the George Washington Bridge from New Jersey into New York City and took the Westside Highway south along the Hudson River all the way down to the financial district at the southern tip of Manhattan. My research sat beside me, untouched.

There were two voices echoing in my head.

Your father is not your father.

Your mother had an affair? No way!

My cousin and my wife were both convinced of their respective positions. For Doug, the science did not lie. My Y chromosome did not match his, and there could be only one explanation: what geneticists delicately refer to as a "non-parental event." In simple terms, my mother had strayed. But for Cindy, just knowing my 94-year-old mother as she did was enough to tell her there had been a mix-up at the DNA lab. Mom had been a shy teetotaler her whole life, raised by a puritanical father and a devoutly Christian mother. She went to church every Sunday, and she read her Bible every day. She was not the type to even look at another man, much less. . . . One of the voices in my head had to be wrong. Either there had been a mistake with my DNA test or my mother was not the person we all thought she was.

I watched the familiar sights go by as my car made its way down the west side of Manhattan past the West 79th Street Boat Basin, then the Intrepid Museum, then Chelsea Piers. It was a beautiful fall day in the city. Puffy white clouds drifted through the blue sky and temperatures were cooling but still comfortable. But I was too distracted to enjoy any of it. The initial shock of Doug's e-mail was still very strong. I felt numb and disconnected.

When we were a few blocks from the stock exchange, I checked my Blackberry and found another message from Doug:

Bill, I apologize for being so blunt in my previous post this morning. . . . Very sorry.

I smiled.

No need to apologize, Cousin . . . :), I wrote back.

Unsettling, yes. I have to believe there's something amiss in the testing process, but we'll get to the bottom of it one way or the other.

I was putting on a good face, just like I did on television. But inside I was feeling a dark emptiness.

The car dropped me off at the corner of Broadway and Wall Street, the most historical part of New York. Dutch merchants who came to the area in the mid-1600s called their colony New Amsterdam. During my genealogical research I had discovered that my ninth great-grandparents, George and Rebecca Woolsey, were married here in 1647, and for a number of years they lived on a small farm at what is now 70 Pearl Street, just a few blocks from the New York Stock Exchange. The Woolseys were ancestors of my paternal grandmother, Mabell Woolsey Griffeth. On days when I had a few extra minutes, I walked the old cobblestone streets that are still just as the Dutch laid them out in the 1600s, enjoying the knowledge that my ancestors had walked these same streets. Occasionally I grabbed a hamburger from the fast food joint that sits precisely on the spot where the Woolsey farmhouse used to be, and savored my secret connection to the area as I ate.

But now as I walked down Wall Street toward the New York Stock Exchange, all I could think about was the DNA test. If it was correct, then I had no connection to this area after all. I was no more related to George Woolsey than I was to George Washington. And I was heartbroken.

The next two hours were a blur. Inside the stock exchange my makeup was applied. I finished reading my research as TV lights were being turned on and microphones were checked. Maria Bartiromo hurried onto the set with her usual rush of energy.

"Hey," she greeted me as she set her bag down, "what's going on?"

Oh, I found out that my father may not have been my father.

"Not much," I said.

At three o'clock, it was show time.

"Welcome to the *Closing Bell.* I'm Maria Bartiromo at the New York Stock Exchange."

"And I'm Bill Griffeth. Another rally on Wall Street today, despite the continuing debt crisis in Europe . . ."

I smiled and looked confident and spoke with energy, and the hour flew by. Maria and I conducted our interviews with floor traders and money managers about the day's news, and by the close of trading the Dow was up eighty points. At four o'clock the bell rang and the show was over.

I took off my makeup, grabbed my overcoat and bag, and headed out to where my car was waiting to take me to the Wharton dinner. The sun was just sinking below the horizon and the air had a crisp chill to it typical of early October. I settled into the backseat and realized that it had been a whole hour since I had thought about Doug's e-mail, and just like that, I felt the disorienting sting of that bizarre moment all over again.

My driver headed north up the Westside Highway toward Midtown and the hotel where the pre-dinner cocktail reception was just getting under way. I looked over my program notes, but it was impossible for me to focus on the task at hand. I picked up my Blackberry, opened Doug's e-mail again and read it for the umpteenth time.

Your father was not Uncle Charles.

I have given speeches for dozens of historical societies and genealogy clubs over the years. My message has always been the same: Genealogy is the pursuit of truth, and if you choose to begin researching your family's history, you had better be prepared to accept whatever truths you uncover. But now, suddenly, I wasn't sure I could do that myself. What in the world was going to happen next, I wondered. Where was all of this going? Sitting in the back of the car that evening, I had no way of knowing that this was only the beginning of a long journey that would include more startling turns—a journey that would ultimately lead me to the discovery of a deeply unsettling truth. My real truth.

CHAPTER 2

My Family, as I Knew It

November 23, 1961

The Griffeth family, 1961

Clockwise from back left: *Scharlene, Charles, Frances, Barbara, Priscilla, Chuck (with Lady), and me*

I had always thought that my family was a little different, and I was the reason why. Take this photograph from Thanksgiving Day in 1961, for example. That's me in front, on the left. I was the youngest of five children born to Charles and Frances Griffeth. My parents delicately referred to me as their "pleasant surprise." My three sisters and my brother were all old enough to be my parents. In fact my eldest sister, Barbara, had two sons of her own by the time I came along. I was an uncle before I was born. And when this photo was taken my sister Priscilla was pregnant with her third child. In the picture she is glaring at her two young children, who were complaining because Billy got to be in the photo and they didn't. It was confusing.

Even at a young age, I knew I was a novelty. The surprised look on people's faces when my parents explained the situation was very telling, although I didn't initially understand their sly grins when they learned the circumstances of my birth. That came years later, and then when I explained the big age gap between me and my siblings, I told it with my own sly grin. *Good for my parents.*

I know that my mother and father loved each other very much. They had been high school sweethearts in the tiny farm community of Washington, Kansas, where they grew up. Dad was a star athlete on the football and basketball teams, and he sang bass in a barbershop quartet that performed at town functions. Mom was shy and preferred to stay out of the limelight. A few weeks after she graduated from high school, in the summer of 1935, they were married by a judge at the county courthouse. Precisely nine months later, in March 1936, my sister Barbara was born, and she was followed in quick succession by Scharlene in 1937 and Priscilla in 1939. My brother, Chuck, arrived in the spring of 1940 after my folks had moved the family to Los Angeles, which is where I was born many years later in 1956.

My family before I was born, on their San Fernando Valley farm, circa 1948

Left to right: *Charles, Frances, Barbara, Scharlene, Priscilla, and Chuck*

They moved to Southern California just as the local economy was taking off. World War II sparked a boom for the many aircraft manufacturers in the area. Jobs were suddenly plentiful, and people poured into the Los Angeles Basin in record numbers, including Doug's parents, my Uncle Dale and Aunt Opal, who arrived from Kansas with four children of their own in the spring of 1942.

During the 1940s my parents and siblings lived in a pleasant neighborhood a few miles south of downtown. Dad worked as a streetcar conductor on the old Yellow Line of the Los Angeles Railway, and my sisters and brother attended the local elementary school two short blocks from home. Despite the backdrop of the war, it was an idyllic time for my family. My mother once said that the 1940s were the happiest time in her life. She and Dad had made the move from Kansas to Los Angeles, where it never snowed, Dad had a decent-paying job, they had four lively children, and Dad's brother lived nearby with his family. Life was good.

In 1947 Dad got a job with North American Aviation and my family moved to the San Fernando Valley, which was still largely agricultural. The Valley had long been known for its citrus groves and dairy farms, and Hollywood used its rocky foothills as a backdrop for hundreds of classic movies, including *Gone with the Wind* and *Stagecoach,* and for TV westerns like *The Lone Ranger* and *The Roy Rogers Show.*

My folks bought a three-acre farm in the west end of the Valley, in the rural town of Canoga Park, near where many movie stars retreated from the Hollywood grind. Roy Rogers and Dale Evans had a ranch a few miles to the west. Lucille Ball and Desi Arnaz owned a home to the east, very close to Lionel Barrymore's place and near the large ranch owned by Barbara Stanwyck and Robert Taylor. Stan Laurel also lived nearby.

Mom and Dad led a life that was familiar to them from their days in Kansas, raising dairy cows and chickens and four energetic teenagers. To bring in more income, Mom went to work for a local nursery. It was a perfect job for her. She loved plants and flowers. She knew the name of every shrub and tree in the area, and she had the greenest thumb I have ever known. Everything flourished under her watchful eye.

By the mid-1950s the San Fernando Valley's population was growing rapidly and new housing developments were quickly replacing farmland. In 1955 my parents sold their farm and moved into a suburban tract home in Reseda, the town made famous by Tom Petty's song "Free Falling" ("It's a long day, livin' in Reseda . . .") and infamous as the fictional porn capital in the motion picture *Boogie Nights*.

Not long after they moved, my parents welcomed their fifth child.

Lady and me, at home in Reseda, California, circa 1963

I was born in the summer of 1956, two weeks after my parents celebrated their twenty-first wedding anniversary. Dad was 42 and Mom was a few months shy of 39. Years later my mother confessed with a blush that her doctor had assured her that she was going through the change of life so she and Dad didn't need to use birth control anymore. Obviously, he was wrong. Just as they were entering middle age and their four children were leaving the nest, my folks suddenly found themselves changing diapers again for the first time in sixteen years.

My childhood was very different from my sisters' and brother's. They were *The Waltons* and I was *Dennis the Menace*. They grew up listening to the radio and I watched TV. They were World War II and I was Vietnam. They were members of the so-called Silent Generation, born between 1925 and 1945. *Time* magazine once characterized the "Silents" as hard-working people who pretty much kept to themselves, calling them "unadventurous," "withdrawn," and "cautious." I, on the other hand, was a classic Baby Boomer, one of the entitled generation born between 1946 and 1964 that clogged the nation's public school system, earned college degrees in unprecedented numbers, and insisted on jobs that were personally fulfilling and meaningful.

When my siblings were growing up, Mom and Dad were still kids themselves. While my father worked hard, the family was far from wealthy. My mother had her hands full making all of her children's clothing, tending to the livestock and vegetable garden, and generally keeping things in order. By the time I came along my father was making a good living, and I grew up essentially as an only child in a comfortable middle-class suburb with two settled, mature adults.

There is no question that Dad and I were different people. He was a man's man, and I was the sensitive type. He did not express himself verbally, but I did. He was good with his hands, a skilled carpenter. I most certainly was not. When I took wood shop in junior high school, our assignment was to make a sailboat out of a block of wood, and by the time I was finished, there were so many holes in it that the teacher told me I made a better plumber than a carpenter.

My father showed his love by making things for me. Instead of buying a swing set, he cut up an old truck tire and hung it from a branch of the giant mulberry tree in our backyard. The best thing about it was when you turned it upside down it looked like a saddle. I spent hours riding in that saddle, swinging back and forth pretending to be Roy Rogers chasing bad guys across the dusty plains. When I got older, Dad took the wheels from an old pair of roller skates, attached them to a two-by-four he cut down, sanded, and varnished, and gave me the coolest skateboard on the block.

My father and I loved watching Lakers basketball games on television. During the 1960s we suffered through many heartbreaking losses to Bill Russell's evil Celtics, and we rejoiced when the Lakers finally won the championship in 1972. After Dad built a free-standing basketball hoop in our backyard, I wore out the lawn shooting baskets for hours and hours, imagining myself as the star of my high school team, just as my father had been in the 1930s when his team went to the Kansas state tournament.

But when I got to high school I found, to my horror, that while most of my friends continued to grow, some to well over six feet tall, I stopped at five foot ten. I played basketball in the tenth grade, but because of my size the coaches put me on the B team. My ego couldn't take watching my taller friends play junior varsity, so I quit after one season and transitioned from athletics to the performing arts. I joined the choir, acted and sang in plays, and served as the half-time announcer for our football games.

My relationship with my father began to change as I matured. We had less and less in common as my interests shifted, and I spent more time with my new girlfriend and less time with him. But he continued to build things for me. To accommodate the growing number of books I loved to read, he built me a small freestanding bookcase, a cherished heirloom that I still have.

My mother and I had a much closer relationship. In fact, my first memory in life involves Mom and a piano that sat in the corner of our living room. It was an old upright with a blond wood finish and tarnished metal foot pedals. The tinny sounds it emitted would have been better suited to a smoky Wild West saloon. It definitely did not fit in with the décor of our home, but it remained a fixture until the day it was removed to make way for our first color TV.

When I was very small I would lie on the floor and watch my mother's feet work the piano's pedals as she played. I learned that pressing down on the left pedal created a prolonged echo, extending the sound well past its origins, and pressing the right pedal stopped the sound cold. When I lay on the floor, up against the piano's lower panel, I not only heard the music, I felt it. The notes vibrated through my small body. I was stirred by the eternalness of that echo, floating on each note as it carried me along, and I never wanted it to end.

Mom played hymns out of an old beat-up Methodist hymnal, and she sang as she played. It was on that old piano that I first heard "Amazing Grace," "Onward, Christian Soldiers," and—my grandmother's favorite—"The Old Rugged Cross."

On a hill far away stood an old rugged cross,
the emblem of suffering and shame;
and I love that old cross where the dearest and best
for a world of lost sinners was slain.

As an adult I have heard firsthand the towering sounds of magnificent organs in some of the world's great cathedrals—Saint Paul's in London, Saint Peter's in Rome, Notre Dame in Paris, and Saint Patrick's in New York—and the vibrations they send through me are no different from what I first experienced lying under my mother's honky-tonk piano, listening to her sing the old songs.

Mom gently instilled in me the same strong Christian ethic she was brought up on, which called for obedience and humility—something she learned from her father, who learned it from his mother. Life had many rules. Follow the rules or be punished. And above all, be humble. Never brag about yourself or your achievements. Let others do it for you, she said.

I can picture my mother sitting with me in our local Methodist church on Sunday mornings when I was very young. I especially remember when they served Communion. As the bread plate came by, Mom took two pieces and handed me one. I gently cupped the small white cube in my hand, wondering what I was supposed to do with it. Next the tray of tiny cups filled with grape juice was passed to us, and she took one and handed it to me and then took one for herself. When the minister gave the signal, my mother ate the bread and downed the juice. I watched her and did the same. At moments like that, Mom's face had a solemn expression that I can still see so clearly. It told me that church was serious business. The message was clear: Don't mess with God.

When I was still a small child, Mom formulated a plan for me. She knew her little boy was unlike her first four children, who were constantly in motion. I was quiet and could sit for hours occupying myself with books instead of going outside to play.

Her plan was that I would be the first person in the family to go to college. I was going to be a professional man. She was constantly reinforcing that notion in me. "You will never work with your hands," she often said. "Not like your father." And she got her wish. I was indeed the first person in my family to graduate from college, and for several years my college diploma was the most tangible evidence that I was different from my siblings.

I dearly wish that was still the case.

CHAPTER 3

"You're Still My Little Brother"

October 8, 2012

In the days after I received Doug's e-mail, I felt detached; all I could do was go through the motions. Cindy and I flew to North Carolina and spent a long weekend with our friends in their beautiful home. We played golf, had dinners out, took long drives in the countryside, and talked about our kids—things we had enjoyed doing with them for years. But I wasn't really present for any of it, emotionally. I desperately wanted to slip away by myself and process the shock I was feeling. But I couldn't, and so I dragged my secret around with me like an invisible barbell.

When Cindy and I returned home Monday afternoon I immediately sat down at my computer and looked again at that message:

Your father was not Uncle Charles.

How exactly had Doug reached this conclusion so quickly and so definitively?

Retesting has confirmed that your paternal haplogroup is I1, not the expected R1.

I had no clue what a haplogroup was. I had some research to do.

I remembered from high school biology that each human cell has twenty-three pairs of chromosomes. Twenty-two of the pairs are essentially the same in men and women. The twenty-third pair determines our gender. Women have two X chromosomes, one from each parent, and men have one X and one Y. The X comes from the man's mother and the Y from his father.

Mother	Father	Mother	Father
X	X	X	Y
Female child		Male child	

Geneticists have divided Y chromosomes into broad categories called haplogroups—*haplo* is from an ancient Greek word meaning single or simple—designated by capital letters ranging from A to T.

A distinctive feature of the Y chromosome is that it passes from father to son pretty much unchanged through countless generations. So the Y chromosome my father, Charles, inherited from his father, Curtis, would be identical to the Y chromosome Curtis inherited from his father, Orson, and from his grandfather, Carlos, and so on. In other words, each generation of Griffeth men would have exactly the same Y chromosome.

Five Generations of Griffeth Men

Carlos
Orson
Curtis

Dale		Charles	
Ron	Doug	Chuck	me

The DNA lab said Doug and his older brother, Ron, were R1s. That meant every male in the chart should also be an R1. But the lab said I was an I1.

I scrolled back to earlier e-mail exchanges between Doug and the DNA lab that I had been copied on, e-mails that I had not bothered to read when they first arrived. There was, for example, this note from the lab to Doug in mid-September:

I would recommend doing a retest on Bill because he does not match any other Griffiths [sic] *while you do. Therefore, it's much more likely that if either of your results are wrong it's his.*

Doug had immediately written back, again copying me:

Bill and I are first cousins; our fathers were brothers. The results . . . for Bill and me should be identical. They are far from that; Bill's results look like a different haplogroup entirely! If possible, could you please run Bill's specimen through again? . . . Either Bill's father was not my Uncle Charles, or Uncle Charles's father was not Curtis Griffeth, my grandfather. Or there was a mistake . . . or a switched sample in the lab. Obviously, this is of great importance to me as well, since I promoted [your service] to Bill for over a year before he took the plunge. PLEASE LET ME KNOW THAT YOU ARE GOING TO DO SOMETHING, THE SOONER THE BETTER—THANK YOU!!! Also, DO NOT contact Bill first. If there is a paternity issue, I want to be the one to break it to him. His mother is still alive, and we will have to deal with this with great care.

The warning bells had gone off weeks earlier. They had been right there on my computer the whole time, and I had ignored them.

Then I spotted a new e-mail Doug had received from the lab while Cindy and I were in North Carolina. Once again, I was copied on it.

Hello Doug,

We have appreciated your patience. The retest for [Bill's] kit is now complete. We have verified that the values match the initial test values and his results are therefore confirmed. Please let me know if there's anything else I can do for you.

So the retest did indeed say that my haplogroup did not match Doug's. Was it really possible that the cells I scraped from the inside of my cheek had revealed a secret that had been hidden from me my whole life? I had to be absolutely certain that the DNA lab's stunning results were valid. The only way to do that would be to submit a sample to another lab for testing. And it occurred to me that I should have my brother, Chuck, do the same, to see if he and I matched.

In the meantime I would not allow myself to think about the many questions my DNA test was raising about my father and mother and their relationship. If the results were correct—and I was not at all ready to believe that—there would be plenty of time later to begin asking some very hard questions.

I searched online for another DNA lab. This kind of testing, known as genetic genealogy, was relatively new. It was first offered to the public in 2000. Each test identified a Y chromosome's haplogroup and evaluated microscopic mutations called markers. The cost of a test depended on how many markers on your Y chromosome you wanted to have evaluated. The lowest number of markers a lab would evaluate was 12, and the highest number was 111. The more markers evaluated, the more you learned about your family's gene pool.

When I submitted my first DNA sample in August 2012, I paid to have sixty-seven markers tested. Since Doug and I were first cousins, our Y chromosomes should have matched on virtually all of them. But for my second test, since I was only interested in learning my haplogroup designation, I signed up with a different lab for a test that evaluated only the minimum twelve markers. I entered my name, address, and credit card information and hit the send button. The confirmation said my kit would arrive in two to three weeks.

Next I called my mother to let her know we had gotten home safely from our weekend in North Carolina.

"Hello!" she said when she answered the phone. Her voice was cheerful. She was excited to hear from me. She always was.

"Hello there," I said, trying to sound normal. It was the first time we had spoken since I received Doug's e-mail.

Mom began by asking how the weather was in North Carolina. We always talked about the weather, and it wasn't because we didn't have anything else to talk about. My mother had always been interested in weather. I've long believed it was because she was the daughter of a farmer for whom weather had been a priority, not an afterthought.

I answered all of her questions, and I asked what she had been up to. She lived in an assisted living facility in the Antelope Valley thirty miles north of Los Angeles. She had her own apartment and a group of friends who met daily in the cafeteria, where they ate all of their meals together. At age 94 she was in great shape. I jokingly referred to her as my Energizer Bunny. She just kept going and going.

It was all I could do not to sound distracted as we chatted. Should I say something about the DNA test? *Mom, you're not going to believe this . . .*

If it wasn't true, then we could share a good laugh. But what if it was true? How was she supposed to respond? Should I expect her to admit on the spot that the man I believed was my father wasn't really my father, just like that? And then what? Talk about the weather some more? As much as I wanted to know the truth immediately, I could not do that to my mother. Not when we were three thousand miles apart and she was all alone in her apartment. My question would have to wait. We finished our pleasant, uneventful conversation and hung up.

I badly needed to tell someone about my DNA test. But who? My two eldest sisters, Barbara and Scharlene, had passed away, and my youngest sister, Priscilla, had been estranged from the family for years. I called my brother in California.

"Well, Willie," he said when he answered the phone. "What's going on?"

Chuck and I have had different journeys in life. He grew up on a farm with three older sisters who were always ganging up on him, and I was a suburbanite who lived the quiet life of an only child. I'm a book learner and he's street smart. I'm deliberate and he's impulsive (there is a tattoo of a cobra on his forearm, to prove it—a souvenir from a weekend trip to Tijuana in 1962). He's skilled at working with wood and metal, like Dad was, and I'm not. After high school I went to college and he went to work in a machine shop. He was Bud Anderson on *Father Knows Best,* the energetic teenager who was always getting into mischief, and I was Opie Taylor on *The Andy Griffith Show,* the quiet kid who minded his manners.

Chuck was 16 when I was born. My parents loved to tell the story about how, when Mom went into labor, Dad had frantically helped her into the car and was pulling out of the driveway for the trip to the hospital when Chuck came running out of the house yelling, "Wait! Who's going to make dinner tonight?"

Chuck and me, holding Lady, in our backyard in Reseda, circa 1960

It would have been easy for my brother to resent me. I had replaced him as the baby and the only boy of the family. But that was never the case. He always had my back when I was growing up. As we got older, the age difference between us became less and less significant, and we developed a genuine respect for each other and for each other's accomplishments. He owned a successful business and bred racehorses on his eighty-acre ranch, while I pursued a career in TV news on Wall Street. He wore cowboy boots and I wore wing tips. But we were still brothers.

"So what's going on?" he asked when I called.

Where should I begin?

"You remember the DNA test Doug had me take a couple of months ago?"

"DNA test . . . ," he repeated. I couldn't tell whether he didn't remember or he didn't know what a DNA test was.

"You know, I swabbed my cheek with those Q-tips and sent them to a lab."

"Yes . . . " Now there was apprehension in his voice.

I took a deep breath. "Well, the test came back and it showed that I didn't match Doug."

"And—"

"And, well, Doug says it means that Dad wasn't my father."

"What??" He started laughing. Chuck and I have exactly the same laugh. And even though I wasn't laughing with him, I was comforted hearing that familiar *yuck yuck yuck* sound we both make.

"I know. Crazy, right?" I said, trying to hide my pain.

"I always knew they brought the wrong kid home from the hospital," he said. My brother, always the kidder. Just like Dad.

But he could tell that I was not laughing, and he turned serious.

"How do they know this?" he asked.

I briefly explained what little I knew about haplogroups and how mine didn't match Doug's.

"Haplo-*what?*"

I explained again and he said he understood, but I knew he didn't.

"Have you told Mom?" he asked.

"No. I don't think that's a good idea until we know for sure. Don't you agree?"

"I guess so. Now what?"

"Well, just to be absolutely certain about this," I said, "I'm going to have another test done with a different service. And I think you should have a test done. Just so we know who matches whom."

"Okay," he said. "What do I need to do?"

I told him I would e-mail him the name and address of the first lab I used. I figured there was no harm in his submitting a sample to them.

"Don't worry," he said. "We'll get this straightened out."

"I know," I said. And we hung up.

I got out a pad of paper and a pen and sketched out the possible scenarios this new test could present.

Scenario 1

R1
Doug
Chuck
me

In the first scenario, my second test result would show that I was indeed an R1, the same as Doug, and—presumably—Chuck. So the first outcome was the result of a mix-up in the lab. It was all a big misunderstanding.

Scenario 2

R1	I1
Doug	me
Chuck	

The second possible scenario would be that my second test result would come back the same as the first, meaning I was indeed an I1. Assuming Chuck's test showed he was an R1, the same as Doug, it would mean Chuck and I had different fathers. We were really *half* brothers. Mom would have some explaining to do.

Scenario 3

R1	I1
Doug	me
	Chuck

The third and final scenario was that Chuck and I would both turn out to be I1s, different from Doug's R1. That would mean Chuck and I had the same father and Doug's father, Dale, and our father, Charles, were the ones with different fathers. Then our

Grandmother Griffeth—if she were still alive—would have the explaining to do.

The phone rang. It was my brother calling back. "Something just occurred to me," he said. "What if Dad and Uncle Dale are the ones who weren't related?" His wheels were turning.

"Now you're getting it," I said. "Frankly, I'm more willing to believe that Grandma was the guilty party here."

"Me, too," he said. "Mom fooled around? Are you kidding me?"

We both laughed our matching laughs.

"Hey," he said. "No matter what, you're still my little brother."

"I know." I started to choke up. "You're not going to get rid of me that easily."

CHAPTER 4

Nothing Makes Sense

October 24, 2012

It was nine o'clock on a Wednesday morning in late October, less than a month after Doug told me about my DNA test. I had been up for a couple of hours. I had had my breakfast and my two cups of coffee. I had read the paper, read my e-mail, checked the Internet for political and economic news and to see how the markets in Asia and Europe had done overnight. I was all caught up and ready for the day to begin. Pretty soon I would have to shower and shave and get ready to head to the studio. Instead, I went upstairs and plopped down in the easy chair in the sitting area of our bedroom.

I was exhausted, completely drained of all energy. My body felt like lead. I was conscious of my every breath, and my chest felt like someone was pressing down on it. I let my mind wander, taking me wherever it wanted to go, like a boat unmoored and drifting. I looked out the bay window at the blue sky and the tops of the trees in our yard waving in a gentle breeze. I was numb to all of it. It was like watching a movie with the sound off.

This was not the first time I had experienced this near catatonic state since Doug's e-mail arrived. I was learning that when I felt like this, there was nothing I could do about it. I didn't fight it, but just let it happen. All I was capable of doing was sitting and staring at nothing in particular and simply experiencing my "new normal."

I had not begun to understand the bizarre bend in the road that had altered my view of the world. And Cindy didn't try to pull me out of it. She knew that nothing she said would help. There were no words of encouragement; no attempt to reassure me. What she understood was that this had rocked me to my core, and I was going to have to work my way through this hell by myself.

Pretty soon I would get up and get ready for work, and at three o'clock that afternoon I would do my TV show from the floor of the stock exchange with energy and enthusiasm. No one would be any the wiser. But at that moment, at nine o'clock in the morning on that particular day—one of *those* days—I did not move. I couldn't. All was silent, and I swear I could feel the rotation of the earth.

CHAPTER 5

Grandma Griffeth

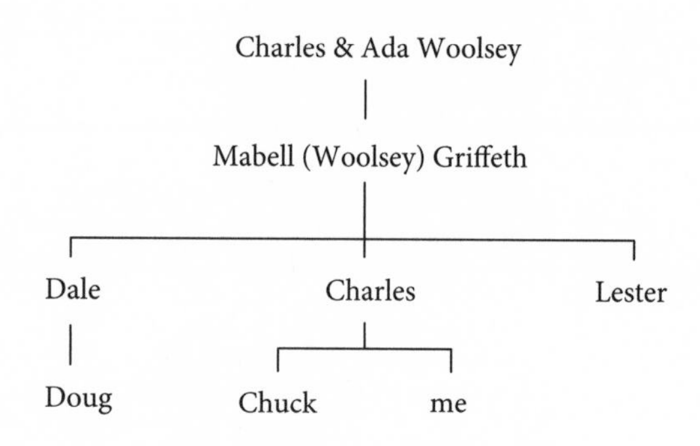

Because of my DNA test result, I found myself asking questions about my family's history that never would have occurred to me before—like, "Could my Grandmother Griffeth have had a secret lover when she was a young married woman?" It was such an absurd question to pose. This was, after all, my beloved Grandma we were talking about. I had countless fond memories of her. When I was a child she lived in Colorado Springs, Colorado, and each summer when my parents and I visited her, she would take us to see the beautiful natural wonders in the area. I remember going to popular tourist attractions with romantic names, such as the Cave of the Winds, Seven Falls, and the massive Royal Gorge. They were like nature's version of Disneyland. When I was in high school she moved to Los Angeles, and for a time she lived in an apartment only one block from my parents' house and attended our local Methodist church with us. Having her live so close was a real treat.

Grandma was 64 years old when I was born, so I knew her only as an old lady with naturally curly white hair, thick eyeglasses, a halting limp owing to arthritic hips, and a persistent cough. Not exactly the sexy seductress type. But what about when she was younger? Nothing I thought I knew about my family could be taken for granted, and so the question had to be asked:

who was more likely to have had a secret lover, my mother or my father's mother? Honestly, I would have to choose my grandmother, because there was, in fact, one person in her life I suddenly wondered about.

My paternal grandmother Mabell Griffeth in Washington, Kansas, circa 1930

Grandma was born Mabell Lena Woolsey in 1892 in the tiny village of Elk Creek, Nebraska, the second of five children born to Charles and Ada Woolsey.

My great-grandfather Charles Woolsey pursued a variety of careers—farmer, furniture retailer, mortician—but none successfully. He moved his wife and five children as he pursued each new opportunity, from Elk Creek to Hastings, Nebraska, and then to Munden, Kansas. In 1905, when Mabell was 13 years old, her mother, Ada, died giving birth to a sixth child, who also died. One year later 36-year-old Charles pursued his next opportunity: he married Angie Pope, age 19, and they went on to have six children of their own.

In October 1910, four days before she turned 18, Mabell married 22-year-old Curtis Griffeth. Curt's parents owned the only hotel in Munden. His three sisters cleaned rooms and served meals, and he and his two brothers did odd jobs around the place, painting this and repairing that.

My great-grandparents Charles and Ada Woolsey (with my grandmother's elder sister, Lynette), in Elk Creek, Nebraska, 1889

After they were married, Curt and Mabell moved to Hastings, where he went to work for the railroad. They had three sons: Doug's father, Dale, born in October of 1911, my father, Charles, born in February 1914, and our Uncle Lester, who came along in March 1918.

In the 1920s, when a prolonged railroad strike threatened to put a lot of men out of work, Granddad quit and moved the family south to Washington, Kansas, where he got a more stable job as a lineman with the local power company.

Granddad Curt was killed in a work-related accident in 1950. For the next eight years Grandma lived a quiet life alone in the house she had shared with Granddad in Greenleaf, Kansas. All of that changed in 1958, when she began a correspondence with Everett Day, an old family friend who had recently been widowed. They were married a year later, in 1959, and Grandma moved to his home in Colorado Springs.

My grandparents Curt and Mabell (Woolsey) Griffeth, in Greenleaf, Kansas, 1946

Everett Day was the only grandfather I ever knew. When I was very young, he and Grandma made frequent trips to Los Angeles, and I remember many times when Grandpa Day walked me to my elementary school in the morning and picked me up in the afternoon. He was a big bear of a man, like my father, and a classy dresser. I picture him waiting for me on the street corner in the afternoon, wearing a khaki-colored Eisenhower jacket and a chocolate-brown fedora, smoking his exotic Tiparillo cigars. I would run to him after school and he would casually extend his index finger, which I'd grab with my own small hand—something I also did with my father—and he would walk me home, asking me how my day at school had gone.

Sometime in the mid-1960s Grandpa Day suffered a debilitating stroke that paralyzed his left side, and the trips to LA stopped. Instead we started visiting them each summer in Colorado Springs, on our way to see other relatives in Kansas.

Everett and Mabell Day, Colorado Springs, 1966

Before his stroke, Grandpa Day drove the Zamboni machine at the ice rink at the famous Broadmoor Hotel. I remember seeing the ice shows there and meeting a young skater who trained at the Broadmoor named Peggy Fleming, not long before she became a legend at the 1968 Winter Olympics.

Grandpa Day didn't live to see Peggy skate in those Olympics. He died just days before she was scheduled to compete, and he was buried in Washington, Kansas, next to his first wife. Grandma then moved to California to be near her sons and their families. She died in 1991 at the age of 99, on the forty-first anniversary of the day Granddad Griffeth was killed, and she is buried next to him in a remote country graveyard not far from Munden, Kansas, where they had met so long ago as teenagers.

Mom once told me that Dad never liked Everett Day. The Days and the Griffeths had, in fact, been friends going back many years. That friendship ended, at least for my father, during the Depression in the 1930s when—according to my mother—Everett "stole" a job from Dad by bribing the employer. As a result, Dad was very upset when Everett Day became his stepfather years later. Of all people.

After my first DNA test result came back and I was left to wonder when a non-parental event could possibly have occurred in my family's history, I took another look at my grandmother's relationship with her second husband and started asking some new questions. Could Everett Day have been my biological grandfather? Was it possible that the man my father held a grudge against for so many years was actually his father?

Dad was born in February 1914 when the family lived in Hastings. I have no idea where Everett Day was at that time. I know he was born in Washington, Kansas, in 1893, but he doesn't show up in the 1915 Kansas state census, which leaves open the possibility that he could have been living in Nebraska at the time. A couple of years after that, during World War I, Everett enlisted in the navy, and by 1920 the U.S. federal census shows that he was stationed at a U.S. naval base in Germany.

So how exactly did my grandmother meet Everett Day? And why did he turn to her so soon after his wife died? They weren't neighbors at the time. He was living in Colorado and she was five hundred miles away in Kansas. Did their letters to each other rekindle a secret relationship from long before?

I believe I found my answer in the 1930 U.S. federal census, which was conducted on Thursday, April 24. I was already familiar with the record that showed the Griffeth family living on West First Street in Washington, Kansas. It listed 41-year-old Curtis, his 38-year-old wife, Mabell, and their three sons: Dale, 18; Charles, 16; and Lester, 12. When I began to research Everett Day's life more closely, I found him in the same census, also living in Washington, Kansas, with his wife, Louisa, her two children from a previous marriage, and Everett and Louisa's daughter, Anita. To my surprise, I found that the Days also lived on West First Street. Right next door to the Griffeths.

There was the connection I was looking for. Grandma Griffeth and Everett Day probably met when they were next-door neighbors in the 1920s (both families showed up at the same location in the 1925 Kansas state census), long after my father was born. And if that was the case, it meant Everett Day was not my father's father. It also meant that it was probably my grandmother who had first reached out to Everett, when she heard that his wife—

and her friend—had died years later in 1958, not the other way around as I had originally assumed.

The idea that Everett Day could secretly have been my biological grandfather was absurd. I knew I had been grasping at straws, conjuring a fanciful tale from a few clues. But it was no more absurd than my unexpected DNA test result. I was left with one last, troubling conclusion. If my DNA test was correct, and my grandmother had not strayed during her marriage, it meant that my mother must have. And that, for me, was the most absurd possibility of all.

CHAPTER 6

Swab Carefully

November 8, 2012

The DNA kit I ordered for my second test arrived in early November. The glossy brochure that came with it promised an "exciting and profound exploratory journey" and an "unprecedented view of your lineage." I opened the package. There were two matching swabs on detachable sticks and two small vials filled with a clear liquid. Just like the test kit Doug had sent me four months earlier in July.

I hadn't paid much attention to that first kit when it arrived. It sat on my desk at home untouched for a couple of weeks. DNA testing did not interest me at all at the time. It was Doug's thing. But then I had spotted the kit one morning in early August, still sitting on my desk. I had forgotten all about it. I was rushing around with a cup of coffee in my hand attending to last-minute details for a trip Cindy and I were taking. We were flying to Kansas City the next day to meet up with Chuck and his wife, Terryll, and with Doug, who were all flying in from California. They were going to join us for a weeklong ancestor hunt I had organized that would take us through the parts of Kansas where our ancestors had lived a century earlier.

I set down the cup of coffee, tore open the package, and skimmed the instructions. "No hot liquids before taking samples," it said. I looked at the cup and at the clock sitting next to it. I had no choice. I had to hurry to get it in the mail before we left, so I hastily scraped the insides of my cheeks, deposited the swabs in the vials, placed them in the envelope, sealed it, and shoved it into our mailbox on the front porch. Then I went back to my packing. At least when I saw Doug the next day I could assure him that, yes, I had sent in my sample.

It was different when the second kit arrived three months later in November. This time I read the instructions more carefully and followed everything to the letter, slowly and precisely, as though

I were disarming a bomb: "Do NOT drink, eat, chew gum, or smoke for at least an hour before taking your samples . . . with clean hands carefully open the plastic wrapper . . . scrape vigorously for 45 seconds . . . eject the swab tip into the vial . . . close the cap of the vial carefully . . . must be shut tightly to ensure the quality of the sample."

When I had completed the operation, I carefully sealed the envelope, drove it to the post office, and handed it to the woman behind the counter. She turned and tossed it on a stack of packages behind her.

I pictured the kit arriving at the testing lab, where some anonymous technician would open the envelope and do whatever the lab does to evaluate the DNA in those vials. Was it like paint-by-numbers, I wondered? Did they simply mix it with some special chemical that turned the liquid into a color that identified the haplogroup, blue for R1, for example, and maybe green for I1? Or did it go under a microscope for a more expert evaluation?

However it was done, the technician would assign a letter and a number, and it would be on to the next sample. And the next. And then it would be time for lunch. All in a day's work.

On my way home from the post office, all I could think about was the fine-print warning I had seen on the DNA lab's website: "You may learn information about yourself that you do not anticipate. This information may evoke strong emotions and has the potential to alter your life and worldview. You may discover things . . . e.g., your father is not genetically your father."

I was not alone, obviously. But I didn't know anyone else who had had this same experience. Or did I? Who else was out there harboring a secret like mine? Had other people also submitted DNA samples thinking the test was an amusing novelty and gotten a punch in the gut in return?

The testing kit said I would receive my results in three to six weeks.

CHAPTER 7

"Families Are Good at Keeping Secrets"

August 4, 2012

Family histories don't often give up their secrets willingly. That's why genealogical research, when done properly, is painstaking and time consuming. And I love everything about it. For me, there is a romance to the tedious grunt work it sometimes takes to uncover what has been hidden for years. I relish the hours I have spent combing through yellowed church and courthouse records in remote villages and the miles I've walked in ancient graveyards, passing by rows and rows of weathered headstones. It is all part of a journey of discovery—and self-discovery.

I especially love what I call ancestor hunts, the field trips to places in the United States and Europe where my forebears lived that allow me to walk where they walked and spend time retracing, reimagining, and reliving. That's when names on a page come alive and the people become real.

I devoted several months in 2012 to planning the ancestor hunt through the parts of Kansas where my family had settled more than a hundred years ago. When I invited Doug and Chuck and Terryll to join Cindy and me, they had all accepted, and it turned out to be a wonderful trip. We spent seven days in early August exploring and reminiscing, oblivious to the DNA tsunami that would hit two months later.

Cindy and I flew to Kansas City International Airport on the morning of August 4. Out the window of the jet we saw the familiar brown and green squares of the heartland. Thousands of years ago this part of the country was covered by a massive lake that eventually dried up, leaving behind miles and miles of flat, fertile bottomland. The Homestead Act of 1862 carved it up into forty-acre squares that the federal government gave away to anyone willing to farm it. Towns sprang up and railroad tracks were laid and a booming agrarian economy was created. But it didn't last. The industrial age lured young people away from their family farms and into cities with factories that paid an attractive wage. Then that didn't last, either. Those industrial jobs went overseas, and the economy moved on. Now many towns and farms remain abandoned and the railroad tracks are rusted.

After we landed, Cindy and I took a shuttle bus to the modern car rental center where Doug was waiting for us. He was easy to spot across the room with his shock of thick white hair, the trademark of most Griffeth men. Our grandfather Curtis had it, our fathers Charles and Dale had it, and Doug's older brother, Ron, also had it. I most certainly did not.

We hugged and compared notes about our flights.

"By the way," I said, "I sent that DNA sample in."

"Good!" Doug said. "The results should be very instructive. Can't wait to see them."

The three of us were talking about the week ahead when Chuck and Terryll walked in. I had first met my future sister-in-law when I was eight years old. It was the summer of 1964 when my big brother brought a young woman home for the family to meet. She was a local girl who had grown up riding show horses in competitions, and as a teenager she had worked briefly as a model. Moments after Chuck introduced Terryll to us, he asked my parents how much cash they had in the house. He needed it because they were on their way to Las Vegas to get married. That was how my brother rolled. Always spur of the moment.

In spite of the impulsive beginning, their marriage lasted. They had a son, Dane, who has always been like a little brother to me, Chuck started his own machine-tool business that was a success for many years, and he and Terryll pursued their passion raising racehorses.

The five of us chatted enthusiastically in the car rental center about our trip. The Griffeth family roots went deep in that part of the Midwest. Chuck's and my parents, and Doug's parents, and all of our siblings were born in this part of the country. Chuck and Doug and I were the only ones born in California. This was our chance to see the homes and farms and graves and other landmarks that were part of our history.

Me, Terryll, Cindy, Doug, and Chuck, in Kansas City, 2012

We rented two cars. Doug rode with Cindy and me, and Chuck and Terryll followed us as we headed west along Interstate 70. The spring wheat had been harvested by that time, and the fields we passed along the way were dotted with rolled-up bales that looked like giant cinnamon rolls.

We stopped in Manhattan and had lunch in a restaurant around the corner from Kansas State University, where many of my mother's relatives had gone to school.

"How did the Griffeths end up in Kansas?" Terryll asked after we ordered our food.

"I'm not certain," I said, "but I suspect it had something to do with their religion."

Our Griffeth ancestors were early members of the Mormon church. Our third great-grandfather, Judah Griffeth, the church elder, had moved his family west in the 1840s with the rest of the church membership, from Ohio to Illinois, where the Mormons founded the town of Nauvoo on the banks of the Mississippi River. That was where Judah and his wife, Mariah, raised their nine children.

"When church founder Joseph Smith Jr. was murdered in 1844," I said, "there was a violent power struggle among his followers and they divided into several splinter groups. The majority of them followed Brigham Young to the Utah Territory, where they settled for good. Most of the Griffeth family stayed behind in Illinois.

Only Judah's eldest son went to Utah and became a very active Mormon."

"*And* he was a polygamist," Doug said. "He had two wives simultaneously and he fathered nineteen children."

"I didn't know that," Chuck said.

Doug smiled. "Families are good at keeping secrets sometimes," he said.

I continued. "In the 1870s, after Judah and Mariah had died, four Griffeth brothers and one Griffeth sister moved en masse with their spouses and their children to this part of Kansas, where they all homesteaded on adjacent farms. That included our great-great-grandparents, Joseph and Mary Griffeth."

"But why Kansas?" Terryll asked again.

"They were members of a splinter group called the Reorganized Latter Day Saints. And for a time this area had many RLDS members. That may have been what lured them here."

"How did you and your parents become Methodists?" Cindy asked.

"Good question," I said. "Our great-grandparents, Orson and Martha Griffeth, were the first Methodists in the family. Orson was Joseph and Mary's eldest son. For whatever reason, he didn't stay with the RLDS church."

We finished lunch and headed north. Our first stop was the town of Washington, Kansas, where our parents grew up. I hadn't been to Washington in years, but when we turned off the highway onto Main Street, it was like I had never left. Memories came flooding back of the many summers I spent there with my parents, visiting relatives who lived on farms in the area. It had been an idyllic time for me. A city boy, I got to milk cows and run through cornfields with my country cousins.

My full name is William Curtis Griffeth. I hated that name when I was a kid. It was too long and formal, and I didn't like the sound of it. My family and friends all called me Billy, which I preferred much more. But every year without fail, on the first day of school, when the roll was called for the first time and the new teacher was trying to match names with faces, we heard "William Curtis," and my friends would howl with laughter at the unfamiliar name. "William Curtis!" they would mock, and I could only sit and take it. It was soon forgotten by my classmates, but I remembered. The sting lingered, and it made me hate my name even more.

I was named after both of my grandfathers, David William Norris and Curtis Orvillo Griffeth. To me, this meant my first name was a middle name and my middle name was a first name. I once asked my mother why they didn't just give me both of my grandfathers' first names and call me David Curtis. "We liked the sound of William Curtis," she shrugged.

Thank goodness for Billy, and later Bill. No one laughed at those names. And so *William* and *Curtis* were hidden away like the good china and they were brought out only for special occasions, like baptism and graduation. The rest of the time I was just Billy or Bill.

Curtis Griffeth, circa 1950, and David Norris, 1914

I never knew either of my grandfathers. Grandpa Dave died in 1946, ten years before I was born, and Granddad Curt was killed in the work accident in 1950. But I have photos of them, two in particular, that are very meaningful to me. They were taken when both men were roughly the same age I am now, meaning their late 50s. Right away, differences are evident. One had a full head of hair and the other was completely bald. One was cleanshaven, the other had a thick Scotland Yard mustache.

And there were other differences. Grandpa Dave was an energetic wanderer, always anxious to try new things. When he was a teenager in the late 1870s, he left the family farm in Nebraska and joined a wagon train traveling to the Black Hills of the Dakota Territory, where gold had been discovered. He spent time in Deadwood when it was still a lawless mining camp. In his later years, when he was a prosperous gentleman farmer, he bought the first car anyone in the area had ever seen. He also had the first radio. The day Calvin Coolidge was inaugurated president in 1925, Grandma Norris rang the "all call" on the old wall phone and all the neighbors picked up, and together they listened on the party line and for the first time heard the voice of a president, courtesy of the Norris radio.

Granddad Curt was neither outgoing nor adventurous. He was quiet and easygoing. Mom once described him as "just a very nice man." He went about his business without ruffling feathers. I imagine he sat quietly while Grandma Mabell did all of the talking. Granddad was not a farmer. He worked for several years as a lineman for the local power company. And he was a skilled carpenter, a talent he shared with generations of Griffeth men.

My grandfathers died a few years apart. On a cold rainy day in March of 1946, when Grandpa Dave was 88, he insisted on planting peas in the small garden he and Grandma tended behind the house they had bought in the town of Washington when they retired from the farm. He caught a chill planting those peas, went to bed with a cold, which then turned into pneumonia, and a few weeks later he was gone.

Four years after that, in October of 1950, when Granddad Curt was 61, he got a call late one Friday afternoon about a power line problem. He and his partner drove to the farm where the line in question was located. While his partner went to turn the power off, Granddad climbed the pole to see what was what.

What happened next remains in dispute. The fact is that Granddad touched the wires before the power had been shut off. He suffered severe burns to his hands, and the electric shock hurled him off the pole to the ground. One story was that his partner was to blame because he failed to turn the power off in a timely fashion. Another was that Granddad was too anxious to get the job completed on that Friday night, and in his haste he touched the wires before the power had been turned off. No one knows for sure what the truth is. He died in the hospital the next morning, just one week after he and Grandma Mabell celebrated their fortieth wedding anniversary.

When I look at the photographs of my two grandfathers, there is no doubt that I was related to Dave Norris. Those are my mother's eyes, the same eyes she gave to me. And that is my bald head.

Curt Griffeth was another story. He was classically handsome in the way all Griffeth men have been, with the full head of hair, the chiseled jaw line, and the dreamboat eyes. I did not share those features. But I didn't dwell on it too much because he and I shared something else that was important to me: our surname.

When we arrived in Washington to begin our ancestor hunt, we drove past the high school Mom and Dad and Uncle Dale attended in the 1930s, and we stopped and took pictures in front of the courthouse where Mom and Dad and Dale and Opal were married, and then we drove out to the house my folks bought in the summer of 1935 on the outskirts of town.

Mom and Dad's house in Washington, Kansas, 2012

They lived there four years, and it was in this tiny two-bedroom house that my three sisters were born. "And just think," I teased Chuck as we stopped out front to take photographs, "this is where you were conceived."

I called Mom on my cell phone to tell her where we were. She told us Dad planted the trees in the front yard that now towered over the house.

For years we had all heard the story over and over about how and why Mom and Dad left this house and moved the family to California. It was the Depression and times were tough, we were told, and the job opportunities were better out west. It was all very *Grapes of Wrath*.

But then we found out that wasn't the whole story.

I remember an afternoon when Mom and Cindy and I were sitting around chatting aimlessly about family history, and Mom told the Kansas-to-California migration story for the umpteenth time, but this time she revealed a different and very personal reason for the move. She admitted that when she learned in the fall of 1939 that she was pregnant for a fourth time, she panicked. She knew her parents and Dad's parents would not be pleased. She was only 21, already had three little girls, and now had a fourth child on the way. How were they going to feed a family of six on Dad's pay as a milkman? Before they revealed their secret, Mom and Dad hatched a plan to move to Los Angeles, where Dad's younger brother, Lester, had recently found work. Jobs were more plentiful in California. That would be their story.

Two weeks before Thanksgiving, they invited both sets of grandparents over for supper in their little white house and broke the news to them that they were leaving Kansas. (They did not reveal that Mom was pregnant again.) According to Mom, all hell broke loose. Her father, my fiery puritanical grandfather Dave Norris, stormed out of the house in disgust, with poor quiet Grandma Marie reluctantly following behind. Grandma Mabell let Mom and Dad have it with both barrels, loudly telling them what a mistake they were making, while Granddad Curt gently tried to calm her down.

But they did not dissuade my parents from leaving. In fact, Dad got a call from Grandma Mabell's older sister, Aunt Nettie, who already lived in Los Angeles. She had heard about their plans, and she asked if they would bring her grown daughter Madeline and Madeline's three children with them. She would help pay expenses. That really sent Grandma Mabell over the edge.

On the Saturday before Thanksgiving in 1939, nine people—three adults and six small children—squeezed into a 1930 Model A Ford and headed for the West Coast. Mom and Dad sat in the front seat with my youngest sister, Priscilla, who was still an infant, in Mom's lap and Barbara and Scharlene huddled at her feet on the floorboard. Madeline and her three small children crowded into the tiny backseat.

They drove south into Oklahoma, where they picked up Route 66 and headed due west, stopping each evening at camps where they slept in one-room cabins that rented for two dollars a night. On Thursday, November 23—Thanksgiving Day that year in California[1]—the little band of Pilgrims pulled up to the California border. The patrol officers on duty stopped them and asked two questions. First: Are you from Oklahoma? "Okies" were not welcome in the state, the officers sternly informed them. At the time, the huge influx of destitute families fleeing the Dust Bowl in Oklahoma were overcrowding the labor camps in California. Fortunately for my parents, the Kansas license plate on their car helped confirm their answer. Second, the officers demanded the name and address of a person waiting for them in California. They could not just show up without a predetermined place to settle. My folks provided them with Aunt Nettie's name and address, and they were waved on. Several miles down the road they stopped in a park in the dusty town of Needles and had an impromptu Thanksgiving picnic before driving on to LA.

---

[1]Although Thanksgiving has traditionally celebrated on the last Thursday of November, in 1939 President Franklin D. Roosevelt declared that it would be the third Thursday, November 23, bowing to pressure from retailers who wanted to extend the Christmas-shopping season. The plan backfired. Twenty-three states, including California, observed Thanksgiving on the 23rd, twenty-three others stuck to the 30th, and Texas and Colorado observed *both* dates. After nationwide complaints about what became known as "Franksgiving," Congress passed a law in 1941 that placed Thanksgiving on the fourth Thursday of November.

Six months later, in May 1940, Mom gave birth to her first son. They named him Charles Jr. It was then that Dad picked up the phone and made a long-distance call to Kansas and broke the news to his parents and his in-laws that they had a new grandchild. Their secret was finally out and they were a safe distance from the family's stunned and angry reaction.

CHAPTER 8

Outlier

November 10, 2012

Dear Bill,

Here's where we stand: if you remain the family "outlier" at haplogroup I1, and Chuck is also an I1, then we know that the "non-parental event" took place one generation earlier, i.e., Uncle Charles's father was not Curtis. If, however, [Chuck] turns out to be haplogroup R1 like [Doug's brother] Ron and me, then your father was not Uncle Charles!

At some point in time, if the second possibility turns out to be the fact, I would suppose that you might want to have a chat with your mom while she's still with us. Your call, of course. But first, we must await your rerun results, and then wait for Chuck's results before that issue might arise.

Just a few things to think about . . .

No matter the outcome, I remain

Your meddlesome cousin,

—Doug

My meddlesome, but well-meaning, cousin was not one to beat around the bush. An "outlier" had been discovered in our family. For him it was all very fascinating. A triumph of science. A long-buried secret had been uncovered by the wonders of DNA. I had to admit it was a compelling story, and if I were Doug I would also find it irresistible, but this was my life we were talking about, not some lab experiment. "Outlier" was a nice way of saying that either my father was illegitimate or I was. One of us was a bastard born out of wedlock.

. . . you might want to have a chat with your mom while she's still with us.

He was absolutely right, but the thought made me want to curl up into a ball. The birds and bees were never discussed in our home. I vividly remember, when I was a kid, the evening my eldest sister interrupted dinner with a frantic phone call to my parents.

"Where's Mom?" Barbara yelled when I answered. The panic in her voice was obvious.

When our mother picked up the other line I heard my sister say, "The boys are asking about sperm. What do I tell them?" Her boys, my nephews, were a couple years older than I was, and they had come home from school that day suddenly full of awkward questions.

The first thing Mom said was, "Billy, hang up the phone!"

My parents never told me what sperm was, and after that episode I knew never to ask. They eventually sent me on a weekend retreat sponsored by our church to learn about the mysteries of life with my Sunday school classmates. Distasteful information lovingly doled out by strangers in a wholesome setting.

The one and only time I remember discussing sex with my mother occurred in the late 1970s when I was 21 or 22 years old. It was a warm afternoon, typical of summer in Southern California, and Mom and I were sitting outside on the back patio at our house in Reseda while Dad was inside napping. A couple of years earlier he had suffered a heart attack that forced him to retire at the age of 62. After that he spent his days watching TV and reading pulp westerns while he waited for Mom to retire from her job as manager of a school cafeteria.

That summer afternoon she unburdened herself to me, telling me how concerned she was about his well-being. She worried that he would go out to his workshop in the garage and overtax himself. She worried that he wasn't eating properly. And she worried about having sex with him.

"I'm so afraid that he's going to have another heart attack right in the middle of things," she confessed out of the blue.

I don't remember what I said in response, but I do remember feeling an overwhelming embarrassment about my mother's confession. I, too, was worried about my father's health, but this was way more than I needed to know. It is clear that my poor mother was simply at her wit's end and she just had to tell somebody about her concerns, even about her sex life with my father. I just happened to be that somebody.

And now more than thirty years later, as my cousin pointed out in his e-mail, there was a high probability that if my DNA test result proved correct, my mother and I were once again going to have to discuss her sex life. Only this time it would involve another man, and I most certainly was not ready to have that conversation.

CHAPTER 9

Chuck's Test Results Arrive

November 17, 2012

The phone rang on the Saturday morning before Thanksgiving. Caller ID showed that it was my brother calling.

"Hello there!" I said, offering our usual greeting.

"Hey," he said quietly. Not his usual greeting.

"What's up?"

"I got the results back from my DNA test."

"What do they say?" I tried to sound upbeat.

"I'm not really sure."

"What do you mean?"

"It's just a bunch of letters and numbers."

"Can you tell what your haplogroup is?" I asked.

"What's that?" He was playing dumb.

"Do you see an I1 somewhere?" *My* haplogroup. Please let it also be his.

"Eye-One . . . ," he repeated slowly as he scanned the page on the screen in front of him.

I closed my eyes.

"I don't see that," he said.

"Do you see anything that says haplogroup?" I asked with my eyes still closed.

"Haplogroup" he repeated. "Yes. I see that."

"And what letter does it say?" I held my breath.

"It says R1. What does that mean?"

Cindy walked in. On a scratch pad in front of me I scribbled *Chuck matches Doug*. She shook her head and walked out.

I explained to Chuck what the results meant. He matched Doug, which he should, but he did not match my first DNA test, which meant we might have had different fathers. But he already knew all of this. He was just playing dumb because he couldn't bring himself to come right out and tell me. It was my big brother's way of protecting me.

Before we ended our call he spoke sincerely.

"No matter what these tests say, you're still my little brother," he said. "That doesn't change." It was the second time he had said this to me, and I was grateful for the sentiment.

We hung up and I stepped out of my office. "Well . . . ," I said out loud to no one in particular. Cindy and our daughter, Carlee, were waiting for me and we hugged. I was self-conscious about the expression I presented to them because I knew they were scrutinizing me carefully. I tried to make it a happy face, but I knew I must look like someone deeply troubled who was desperate to look otherwise.

"We still have my second test results to go, you know," I said in an encouraging tone. I had expected Cindy to say it first. She was always the one to look on the bright side. But she couldn't do that this time. We hugged more tightly and she whispered, "I can't believe it."

The next day, there was a new e-mail from Doug. Chuck had obviously alerted him to his results, and our cousin had gone over them very carefully.

Dear Bill and Chuck,

Below you will see three DNA charts . . . one for each of us . . . showing DNA markers 1–37. They confirm our thinking that Bill had a different father from Chuck, [since Bill had] only 9 matching markers, and 28 misses. By comparison, Chuck and I miss on only 2 [markers].

Chuck and I are designated as R1 and Bill belongs to the I1 haplogroup.

If you have any questions, please don't hesitate to ask.

Happy Thanksgiving!
—Doug

There it was in black and white: thirty-seven DNA markers listed in Doug's e-mail and Chuck and Doug matched on thirty-five of them, as male first cousins should. Chuck and I should have matched on all thirty-seven markers, but we matched on only nine.

Terryll responded to Doug's e-mail almost immediately.

Hi Doug & Bill:

We have a lot to learn about this, but apparently the thing that is clear is that you and Chuck do match and apparently Bill does not (ruling out an error on his original test which is where my bet lies).

Terryll was still holding out hope that my DNA sample had been mixed up at the lab because, like Cindy and me, she just could not fathom that Mom would ever stray.

But Doug thought otherwise. His e-mail response to Terryll was short and to the point:

The error was ruled out by [the retest of Bill's first sample] *that proved the first test to be correct.*

Doug had moved on. He was not waiting for more test results. He was convinced. He knew my mother. He saw the same quiet, pious Christian woman that we did. And we saw the same test results that he did. But we came to different conclusions. He sided with the science, and we were holding out hope that what we knew about my mother was all the proof we needed.

CHAPTER 10

The Mystery of Ansel Griffeth

August 6, 2012

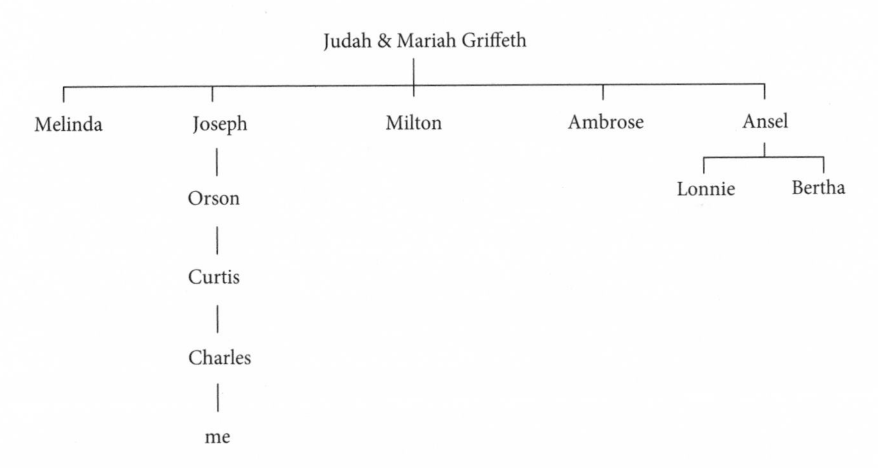

On day two of our August ancestor hunt through Kansas that summer, we were reminded of a tragic secret in our family's history that had been hidden for almost a century.

Family secrets are the buried treasure of genealogy; they're like pearls carefully harvested from ordinary oysters. When I began my own research in the summer of 2003, I learned that my eighth great-grandmother, Mary Towne Estey, was hanged during the infamous Salem witch trials. While abhorring what had happened to her, I was ecstatic to discover that my family had been part of such a dramatic chapter in American history. And what a story: A quiet, devout mother of nine children, minding her own business, is accused of witchcraft. After her conviction, as she awaits execution, she writes an impassioned letter to the authorities—a letter that is now archived in a Salem museum—begging them to stop the madness so that other innocent souls can be saved. Today, Mary and the eighteen others who were executed during that baffling bout of mass hysteria in the summer of 1692 are viewed as heroes, and there are memorials honoring them in Salem and in neighboring Danvers, Massachusetts. And it turns out that being descended from a Salem witch lends an American family tree a certain prestige that is right up there with being descended from a *Mayflower* passenger. For all of these reasons, Mary Towne Estey has been the pearl of my family story, the first person I mention when I describe my family tree.

But since my own DNA issue came to light, I have gained a new perspective on family secrets. Instead of romanticizing them, I now feel a greater compassion for the people directly affected by the tragedies and scandals that were covered up, newly mindful that pearls begin as an irritating grain of sand. As proud as I am of my connection to Mary Towne Estey, I realize that her immediate family would have felt no pride at all. There would have been only fear and shame. Not long after the trials ended, Mary's youngest son, Joshua, moved his wife and children seventy miles south of Salem to Rochester, Massachusetts, no doubt to get a fresh start, away from the stain of his mother's scandalous reputation. Thirty years later, in 1723, when my sixth great-grandfather, Samuel Griffeth, married Joshua's daughter Eleanor Estey, I wonder how much he knew about his bride's disgraced grandmother. Did Eleanor confess her family's ugly secret to her new husband? And if she did, would Samuel and Eleanor then have whispered it to their own children, including my fifth great-grandfather, John Griffeth? Somewhere along the line, someone stopped telling the story and our family's ties to one of American history's most notorious episodes was forgotten. It would be several generations before those ties would be discovered and celebrated.

It is a different story when it comes to the events of April 10, 1920, involving my great-great-uncle, Ansel Griffeth. He will never be famous for what he did. Certainly no monument will ever be built to honor him. And although I once viewed his story as a juicy scandal that raised many tantalizing, unanswered questions, now I see only tragedy. On day two of our ancestor hunt through Kansas, when we were confronted with his story, I did not feel any pride, only sympathy.

It was a blazing hot Monday, typical summer weather in that part of the country, and we were touring the rustic country roads of Republic County in our rental cars, searching for the acreage our great-great-grandfather Joseph Griffeth had homesteaded in the 1870s with two of his brothers and one of his sisters. The Griffeth siblings had moved, all together with their families, from Illinois, where they had been born and raised, to northeastern Kansas near the town of Scandia, presumably to be near other members of the Reformed Latter Day Saints Church, and because land in Kansas was cheaper and more readily available.

To help us find the Griffeth farms, we enlisted the aid of a local researcher I had worked with before on various genealogical projects. And on this miserably hot summer day he led us in a three-car caravan in search of our ancestors' homesteads.

We began the day at their final resting place, the tiny, remote Poplar Grove Cemetery just east of Scandia, a square acre of green grass and weathered headstones surrounded by miles of farmland. Reluctantly, we got out of our air-conditioned cars and explored the small graveyard as the stifling heat and humidity pressed down on us. Cindy and Terryll wisely huddled under some shade trees while Doug roamed the far corners of the property and Chuck and I walked along the rows of graves, studying each name as we went. This was a unique experience for me. It was the first ancestral graveyard I had visited where all of the relatives buried there spelled our surname the same way—Griffeth, instead of the more common Griffith.

The name Griffeth is Welsh. In one translation, it means "great faith." In ancient times it was a man's first name, and it was spelled many ways, including "Gryfudd" and "Gruffudd." As it migrated east onto English soil it became a surname with several variations in spelling, including "Griffiths," "Griffith," and "Griffin."

My earliest known ancestor, our eighth great-grandfather William, spelled it "Griffith." William lived with his family on Cape Cod in the 1600s. He was among the earliest American Quakers to live among the Pilgrims who dominated Plymouth Colony. Quakers were not always welcomed by the colonists. They were often harassed for their beliefs by their neighbors and fellow townspeople, and in a few extreme cases they were hanged.

In the early 1700s, town records started to show the family's name spelled "Griffeth." But not every time: sometimes it was still spelled "Griffith." After a careful inspection during my genealogical research, I came to the conclusion that the spelling change was the work of William's son, my seventh great-grandfather, William Jr. But why did he change the spelling of his name from Griffith to Griffeth? Was he trying to distance himself from his controversial Quaker heritage? Was there some dispute in the family? We don't have that answer. Today there are dozens of family members buried in graveyards in southern Massachusetts, and in some cases a Griffith lies right next to a Griffeth, sometimes within the same immediate family.

But not in Poplar Grove Cemetery. There, everyone was a Griffeth. Chuck and I came upon a pair of matching headstones:

Headstones of Carlos and Mary Griffeth,
Poplar Grove Cemetery, near Scandia, Kansas

"Who's Carlos?" Chuck asked.

"Our great-great-grandfather." I said.

"I thought his name was Joseph."

"It was."

"So who's Carlos?"

"His full name was Joseph Don Carlos Griffeth," I explained, "but everyone called him Carlos. He was named for the founder of the Mormon church, Joseph Smith Jr. His middle name came from Joseph's youngest brother, Don Carlos Smith, who was a prominent leader of the early church."

We moved on, passing by more headstones, and I pointed out other relatives. There was our great-great-uncle Ambrose Griffeth and his wife, Jennie; our great-great-aunt Melinda Griffeth Taylor and her husband, Charles. And at the end of a row, we stopped in front of a modern oversize headstone of black granite.

Ansel and Phebe Griffeth's headstone,
Poplar Grove Cemetery, near Scandia, Kansas

"This is our great-great-uncle Ansel," I explained. "He was Carlos's youngest brother."

"A tragic figure," Doug said as he joined us. "His was one of those stories no family likes to talk about."

We motioned for Cindy and Terryll to join us. The five of us gathered in front of Ansel's headstone and I told them about this dark family secret.

My great-great uncle Ansel Griffeth, in
Warren County, Illinois, circa 1870

Like me, Ansel was the baby of his family. He was Judah and Mariah Griffeth's ninth child, born in 1848 in Fulton County, Illinois. In 1850, when Ansel was 2 years old, his mother died, leaving him to be raised by his cranky 55-year-old father. It is likely, though, that Ansel was actually raised by his older siblings. He was especially close to his brother Milton, who returned from the Civil War suffering from an injury that left his legs virtually useless. For the rest of his life Milton struggled to walk with the help of two canes. When Milton married Mary Creighton in January of 1870, 21-year-old Ansel moved in with them, and for eight years he worked his disabled brother's farm. In 1879 Ansel married a neighbor girl, Phebe Rubart, and followed his brothers and sister to Kansas, where he homesteaded eighty acres next to land that Milton claimed.

Ansel and Feba, as she was called, had two children, a son named Alonzo (called Lonnie) and a daughter, Bertha.

The Ansel Griffeth family, circa 1890

They were an especially close-knit family who kept to themselves. Both Lonnie and Bertha shared their father's shy sensitive nature, and they lived with their parents well into adulthood. Feba's death in 1914 no doubt pulled the remaining family even closer together. Lonnie did not marry until early 1920, when he was 38 years old, and he brought his bride Goldlena home to the family farm to live with his sister and widowed father. Ten years later, in 1930, when Bertha was 46 years old, she married Goldlena's brother George.

The defining moment for Ansel's family occurred on April 10, 1920. Late that Saturday night in the early spring, after everyone had gone to bed, Ansel grabbed a lantern and headed out to the barn, carefully stepping through the patches of snow still on the ground from a late-season storm that had hit the week before. Inside the barn, as the dim yellow light cast distorted shadows on the walls, he took a rope and struggled to climb into the hay wagon inside the barn, not an easy task for a frail 72-year-old man.

Once he had steadied himself, he looked up and began trying to toss one end of the rope over the rafter directly above him. It may have taken a few attempts, but eventually the rope looped over the rafter and fell back to him. He tied it off and slowly and deliberately wrapped the other end around his neck until it was secure. Then, while his adult children slumbered peacefully in their beds, he quietly stepped off the wagon.

The obituary published in the local paper did not say how Ansel had died. In the flowery language typical of the time, it offered the Griffeth family "the sympathy of an immense circle of friends who mourn the passing of an excellent friend," and speculated that "the faithful wife [who] preceded him [in death] by some six years . . . will assist in the welcome at the gates of glory."

After a coroner's inquest was completed, the uncomfortable truth emerged: "Death came by Mr. Griffeth's own hand." A newspaper article revealed that Ansel had not been feeling well and that there had been "domestic troubles," without specifying what they were. The week before his death, Ansel had bumped into a friend on the streets of Scandia. The friend recalled in the article, "We met him on the street and spoke to him as usual, asking him how he was and his answer was, 'Something strange has come over me. I have no sense,' and gave us a look and a grip of the hand that we will not soon forget." This friend told the reporter that "Mr. Griffith [*sic*] had this act in contemplation for some weeks and he told the family and one or two of their neighbors that he would end his life in this manner."

If Lonnie and Bertha knew why their father hanged himself, they never said. Had they expected it? Had he really threatened weeks before to take his life? And if he had, was it dismissed as simply the idle chatter of an old man?

There was the mention in the newspaper of "domestic troubles." What were they? One article said Ansel had agonized over the deteriorating condition of his farm and orchard. Apparently it had become too much for him and Lonnie to handle by themselves. But was that reason enough to kill himself, or was there something more serious going on?

I'm still puzzled about what he meant when he told his friend on the street, "Something strange has come over me. I have no sense." Did Ansel suffer from mental or emotional conditions the family wanted to keep hidden? Was he still depressed about the death six years earlier of his beloved Feba? Or was he experiencing what we now know as the early stages of Alzheimer's disease?

Ansel's family is all gone now. Bertha, who never had any children, died in 1959. Lonnie and Goldlena are also both long gone, and their only child, a daughter named Pearl, died in 1988. The trail has gone cold. The true reason for Ansel's shocking final act will remain a secret buried with him in that lonely graveyard in Kansas.

"I think we're going to turn left up ahead," Cindy said. She was in the backseat of our car, studying a map on her iPad as our little three-car caravan, with our researcher friend leading the way, bounced along yet another dusty country road. After our visit to Poplar Grove Cemetery in the morning we had eaten lunch in Scandia, where we lingered awhile over a second glass of iced tea and chatted about what we had been seeing. Then we resumed our hunt for the abandoned Griffeth farms. The sun was high overhead and there wasn't a breath of air, which added to the heat's intensity. All around us was the constant, high-pitched rattle of male cicadas searching for females to mate with.

We did indeed turn left at the next corner, and as we did our guide slowed, rolled down his window, and pointed to his left. We had at last come upon the place we had been seeking. The Griffeth siblings had homesteaded their adjacent eighty-acre lots here, and lived side by side, farming this land and raising their families, for more than forty years. The farms had long ago been abandoned. Now there were only acres of overgrown switchgrass and a random tree here and there.

We slowly paraded past what had once been the farm of our great-great-aunt Melinda Griffeth Taylor and her husband, Charles. A half mile down the road was the farm of our great-great-grandparents, Joseph and Mary Griffeth. Then the farm of our great-great-uncle Milton Griffeth and his wife, Mary, and finally the corner lot, which had belonged to our great-great-uncle Ansel Griffeth and his wife Feba.

We stopped in front of Ansel's property. Off in the distance was a cluster of tall trees hovering over the remains of an old building.

"I wonder," Doug said. He looked at me. "Do you think it could be?"

Before I could answer, he was out of the car and wading into the tall grass. I got out and started to follow him.

"Where's he going?" Chuck asked as he got out of his car.

"It looks like there's an old building over there in the trees," I said.

Cindy and Terryll stayed behind in the air-conditioned cars while my brother and I made our way carefully through the sea of grass, always on the lookout for the snakes our researcher and guide had warned us about when we began our day. Up ahead, Doug raced on, undaunted.

"What's with the building?" Chuck asked.

"I guess Doug thinks it might have been Ansel's barn," I said.

"*The* barn?"

"Maybe."

We stopped a safe distance away, maybe thirty feet, from the ramshackle structure hiding in the cluster of trees. The roof sagged under the weight of the overgrown branches. Any paint that may have covered its walls had long ago peeled away, leaving exposed rows of warped, brittle boards, discolored after years of assaults by the elements. The building might not have been old enough to have been around in the 1920s, but it was a wonder that it was still standing.

There was no way to get inside; the large door was held shut by a rusted padlock. Doug had positioned himself along one wall, practically waist deep in the grass, and was peering in through a dusty window.

"What do you see?" Chuck called out.

"You're not going to believe this," Doug answered back.

We waited while he took pictures with his cell phone through the window. When he finished he walked back to us.

"Well," I said, "What do you think? Is this the barn?"

"Hard to say for sure," he said. "But take a look at this."

He handed me his phone and I squinted at a photo on the screen, trying to shade it from the sun's glare with my free hand.

"What do you see?" Chuck asked me as I swiped the screen to view a second photo.

I handed him the phone.

The first photo showed the interior of what was clearly a barn. An empty barn. No wagon, no tractor, nothing. It probably hadn't been used for years. In the second photo, Doug had taken a close-up of the ceiling. And there in the shadows, incredibly, was a rope draped over the rafter.

"There is no way that's the rope he used," Chuck said as he handed the phone back to Doug.

"Oh, I agree," Doug said. "But how odd to see something like that after we had just been talking about Ansel's suicide."

This creaky old building may or may not have been the barn. The original had probably been torn down long ago, at the same time the farmhouse was, and replaced by this structure. But still, this had to be the spot where our great-great-uncle had taken his life almost a hundred years ago.

The three of us remained there a while longer. Chuck and Doug continued to speculate about the age of the barn, pointing at this and that feature as they did. I stood quietly and took in the scene, all the while thinking about family secrets.

CHAPTER 11

"I'm Done with This Whole DNA Thing"

November 23, 2012

I was anchoring my show on CNBC on the Friday after Thanksgiving, and as usual on that day, the markets were very quiet. During a commercial break I checked my personal e-mail. There was one from a name I didn't recognize. I opened it.

Hi Bill,

My name is Steve, and I live in Seattle. I work in asset management and was bored in the office so I started combing through some of my DNA matches on [the DNA website]. I had a surreal moment while watching you live on CNBC while simultaneously seeing on my computer that we were somehow related.
Just wanted to say hi to a long lost cousin.

Take care.
Steve

My stomach tightened. *No!* I wanted to shout. *Go away! It's all a big misunderstanding*. This fellow had gained access to my e-mail address through the DNA lab's website. Customers are able to control how much of their personal information is made public, ranging from total anonymity to full disclosure. I had chosen to allow only my email address to be displayed.

I logged on and found Steve's name in the section that listed people who matched my results. It showed that he and I matched on only the first twelve genetic markers of our Y chromosome, which meant we would have to go back several generations to find a common paternal ancestor. As time went on, I would come to understand that twelve-marker matches were a dime a dozen. A match of sixty-seven or more markers was more significant, signaling a much closer relationship. At twelve markers, my new friend Steve and I were barely related. But it was still more markers than my own brother and I shared.

Was this how it was going to be? Would I start hearing from other strangers who were anxious to connect with newly discovered "relatives"? I was not ready for this. I didn't belong here, I thought. I didn't *want* to belong here. I had no interest in corresponding with any of these people. We were getting ahead of ourselves. The results of my second DNA test still hadn't come back, and when they did I was certain they would prove that the first test results were wrong, and all of these people listed on the website would go away.

As a courtesy, I decided to humor this fellow Steve. I hit Reply.

Hey Steve, Nice to hear from a long lost relative. See you at the next reunion.

Cheers,
Bill

I never heard from him again.

But my DNA issue kept coming up at random moments. Two days later Carlee called from Los Angeles. "You're going to love this," she said.

At the time, Carlee was living in LA, where she had a college internship at the Warner Brothers movie studios. When she called, she had just come from taking my mother out for a pleasant Sunday brunch.

"When we got back to Grandma's apartment," Carlee said, "we ran into one of her neighbors. Her name is Jan." Carlee laughed.

Mom often talked about her friend Jan. They ate all of their meals together in the assisted living center's cafeteria.

"What's so funny?" I asked.

"After we said good-bye to her friend, Grandma whispered to me, 'Jan and I tell each other all of our secrets.'"

I got my daughter's joke. *Was I one of those secrets?* But I didn't laugh.

Clearly I was on pins and needles waiting for my test results to come back. In the meantime, it seemed that everywhere I turned I was being reminded of my troubling paternity issue. One day it was an e-mail from a stranger who believed he was my relative, and the next it was my daughter telling me my mother claimed she had secrets.

I had had enough. I called my brother.

"I'm done with this whole DNA thing," I told him. "I don't want to know who my father is."

"What are you talking about?" Chuck asked.

"I mean I already had a father," I said, "and I don't need to go looking for another one."

"So what are you going to do?"

"The way I feel right now, I just want to let sleeping dogs lie. Even if you and I don't match when my second test comes back, it's going to do more harm than good if I start asking a bunch of embarrassing questions. The only father who matters to me was Dad. And I keep thinking about what this would do to Mom. I picture me sitting in her living room, and when I tell her what we've discovered it just shakes her to her core. You know how sensitive she is. If you or I even look at her funny, she thinks we're mad at her. She cares deeply about what we think of her."

"I know."

"Can you imagine what she'll be like if she finds out that we know she fooled around? It will crush her. I can't do that to her. I don't want this to define her final days."

"Yeah, but what if you change your mind and want answers after she dies. Then what?"

"I'll just have to live with that," I said.

"I think you'd better think about this some more. I get what you're saying, but I think you'll live to regret it if you wait too long to start asking questions. And you need to think about Chad and Carlee, too."

I had thought about Chad and Carlee, and Chuck was right. They deserved a vote in the matter. But they had never known Grandpa Charles. He died a year before Chad was born and three years before Carlee's birth, which was probably why they were not so troubled about my rogue DNA test. They did not feel the same degree of loss that I did. And it even went beyond Chad and Carlee. Future generations of our family deserved to know the truth, no matter how uncomfortable it made us feel. I had spent years uncovering family secrets, like Ansel Griffeth's suicide, and I wasn't going to be responsible for yet another cover-up. But it was still too soon to be asking awkward questions. We needed my second DNA test to come back.

What was taking so long? The lab I sent my second sample to had said I could expect results three to six weeks after they received my package. I first started logging on to their website in early December, at the three-week mark. On the home page I clicked on "Check Your Results" and it asked for the personal ID they had issued to me, a long series of letters and numbers. I carefully typed them in, hit Enter, and was redirected to a page that showed a progress report on my sample. There were five steps listed:

RECEIVED PROCESSED TESTED ANALYZED VERIFIED

My sample was still in the "received" category. By mid-December, more than a month after they would have received my sample, it had only moved up to "tested." Halfway there. This was the worst part—the waiting, the wondering, the not knowing. At least it wasn't a health issue, I told myself. We weren't talking about anything life threatening. But we were talking about something life changing.

Just tell me what my haplogroup is and I'll go away!

It didn't take long before I realized that I was going to need some help getting through all of this, so I made an appointment with my doctor. I have never been a fan of doctors, and I go only when it's absolutely necessary. But this doctor I liked. Cindy had found him a few years after we moved from Los Angeles to New Jersey in the early 1990s. He was easy to talk to, and we got along well. In 1999, after an especially arduous road trip for the TV show I was hosting at the time, I came home exhausted, got very sick, and came down with pneumonia. I was off work for almost two months. I had never been that sick before. This doctor got me through it, and when I was on my feet again I went back to him for a complete physical. Voluntarily. Cindy could tell you how unusual that is for me. The trauma of what I had been through had scared me enough to send me in for an overhaul.

That's how I felt when I called his office this time. I was out of other options.

When I arrived for my appointment, he greeted me with a welcoming handshake and invited me into his office so we could chat. The room was warm and comfortable, with thick carpeting on the floor, low mood lighting, and photos of his family everywhere. I was meant to feel calm and reassured, and I did. As we were seating ourselves he remarked on how long it had been since we had last seen each other: eight years. I remembered it had been in 2004, when I tore a calf muscle running up and down a basketball court while I was coaching Carlee's seventh-grade team.

He asked how I was doing.

"Life has been a struggle to get through lately," I told him.

His eyes got really big. He had not expected this.

Our chat lasted forty-five minutes. We never actually got around to the physical exam. I poured my heart out and told him about the events of October 4 and my cousin's e-mail, and all I had been through since then, especially about the catatonic episodes, and the agonizing wait to find out who my biological father was. He took lots of notes.

"You have two choices," he finally said to me. "I can help you find a psychologist who will help you work through this, or I can prescribe an anti-anxiety medication."

He told me he thought seeing a psychologist would be the better route; it would offer a longer lasting solution. But I chose the pills. I was desperate for immediate relief. He scribbled out a prescription and handed it to me. Cindy had it filled while I was at work that afternoon, and I took the first pill the next day with my morning coffee.

I am aware that there is such a thing as a placebo effect. If you think a medication will help you, the chances are greater that it will. My father had been something of a hypochondriac. He was always running to the doctor for one thing or another. On one occasion, Mom whispered to me that Dad had been given sugar tablets to help whatever he thought was ailing him. And they had worked.

I knew that the little white pills I started taking every morning were not sugar tablets, but I had already convinced myself that they were going to help. They had to. I was at my wit's end. Since Doug's first e-mail about the DNA test had showed up in my in-box six weeks earlier, I'd felt like I was operating without any oil in the engine and all of my gears were grinding against each other.

Thirty minutes after I popped the first pill I distinctly felt a sense of relief come over me, as if my body had been lowered into a warm bath. My muscles—and my mind—relaxed. Just like that. Had the medication really worked that quickly, or did I feel this way because I was so anxious for it to work? Was I, in effect, experiencing a placebo effect with real medicine?

I didn't care. It worked. That was all that mattered.

CHAPTER 12

Losing My Father

December 7, 1988

It is never good news when the phone rings at 2:30 in the morning.

"Hello?"

"Hello, Bill. This is Pastor Floyd." My parents' minister. It was the early hours of December 7, 1988. Cindy and I were still living in Los Angeles, and my mother and father were one hundred miles north of us, living out their retirement in the high-desert town of Tehachapi.

"It's about your Dad," Floyd said. He sounded tired and spoke in a whisper. "He's had a heart attack. We're at the hospital, and it doesn't look good. They've asked your mother if she wants to put him on a ventilator. She wants your opinion. Are you ready?"

Was I ready? I thought. *For what, exactly?*

Mom came on the line.

"Billy—" She hadn't called me that in years.

"Hi, Mommy." Instinctively we had both reverted to nicknames we used when I was a child.

"I didn't know what else to do," she said plaintively. She sounded distressed and exhausted.

"I know, sweetheart. It's okay."

"What do you think?" she finally asked.

"Dad wouldn't want to be put on a ventilator."

"They say he would just be a vegetable."

"Then let's not do it," I said. "Dad wouldn't want it that way."

Truthfully, I had no idea what my father would have wanted. But at that moment I was more interested in comforting my mother. Clearly, she didn't want to carry the burden of this decision by herself.

"Thank you," Mom said. "Would you call Scharlene and tell her?"

"We're coming up, Mom," I said.

"Okay. Chuck's on his way, too."

"I love you, Mom."

"I love you, too."

I called my sister and she followed us out to Mom and Dad's.

The drive to Tehachapi took roughly two hours. It was a pitch black night, and we drove in silence, both of us lost in our thoughts. I was kicking myself. Cindy and I hadn't made it to Mom and Dad's for Thanksgiving two weeks earlier. For more than a year we had been trying to have a baby. Cindy's doctor had tried all of the newest techniques to aid conception, to no avail. And then, miraculously, in September she was suddenly pregnant without any medical intervention. We were ecstatic. But our excitement didn't last long. A few weeks later Cindy started having terrible abdominal pains. She was ordered to bed, but the pains only got worse. Finally, her doctor discovered the terrible truth: it was an ectopic, or tubal, pregnancy. He immediately rushed her into surgery and terminated the pregnancy, which left us both emotionally drained and heartbroken and Cindy in a great deal of physical pain. As a result, she had not been up for the two-hour drive out to my family's Thanksgiving celebration. We assured everyone that we would see them at Christmas.

We turned the radio on to fill the silence and to keep us awake.

"Our top story this hour," the news anchor read, "the death of legendary singer Roy Orbison. Dead of a heart attack at the age of 52." Since it was the middle of the night, it was the only story they had, and they reported it over and over again. I turned the radio off, and my thoughts turned to my father, who had just had his own heart attack.

Dad may have been a hypochondriac but he'd also had legitimate health problems—big ones—that materialized like clockwork every ten years. In 1966, when I was 10 years old, his doctor discovered a tumor on one of his lungs. Like many men of his generation, Dad had been a smoker since he was a teenager, and the doctor believed the smoking had caused the tumor. The lower half of Dad's right lung was surgically removed. In those days, minors weren't allowed to visit patients in hospitals, so Mom walked me around the outside of the building so that Dad and I could wave at each other through the window. He smiled at me and I smiled back, but I remember being afraid. I wasn't used to seeing him look so frail and vulnerable. The surgery left him with a big ugly scar that went down his back and around his side. It looked like a snake riding piggyback. The whole episode shook him badly enough that he quit smoking, cold turkey, and he never looked back.

Ten years later, in 1976, Dad was felled by his first heart attack. It happened on a sunny Sunday afternoon in the fall. My girlfriend at that time and I were returning from a shopping trip to the mall. We turned the corner onto my street and saw the flashing red lights of a fire truck and an ambulance at the other end of the block. As we got closer, it became clear that they were in front of my house. We parked on the street and got out. Mom came running through the front door sobbing, and we hugged.

Inside the house, Dad was lying on the floor in the dining room. The table and chairs had been pushed out of the way and two EMTs were kneeling on either side of him talking in stage whispers about pulses and heart rates. I moved in for a closer look and saw a vacant expression on my father's face that alarmed me. He was only 62 years old. Once they had him stabilized, they rolled Dad out on a gurney and loaded him into the ambulance. We jumped into our car and followed him to the hospital.

Dad never really recovered. He had to retire after that, and for the next four years he sat around the house until Mom retired. In the spring of 1980 they bought a small farm in Tehachapi, and in June they left LA for good.

Finally, in 1986, came Dad's last illness: Alzheimer's. I had not heard the word until the evening Mom called to tell us what the doctors said about his recent strange behavior. He had started saying odd things, repeating himself, and generally acting confused.

Around that time, I did an interview with longtime TV personality Art Linkletter about a book he had written called *Old Age Is Not for Sissies.* During a commercial break, I told him about Dad's condition. Not a lot was known about it at that time, but we knew it was not good. Mr. Linkletter shook his head. "You'd better pray that his heart gives out before the disease progresses too far," he told me.

I think back on an afternoon in the summer of 1988. Cindy and I had bought a home in Northridge, California, near where we had both grown up. Dad and I were sitting on our deck, just the two of us, surveying the backyard and enjoying each other's company. He was repeating things he had said before, but he kept saying them as if for the first time. I just listened.

"They gave me a mental test," he told me for the umpteenth time, "but first they gave me these drugs that made me hallucinate. That's why I failed the test. It was the drugs! There's nothing wrong with me!"

I knew what was coming next.

"Do you know what they did? They took away my driver's license. They won't let me drive my own car! Can you imagine?" This was the greatest of indignities for my father, not being able to drive. He took great pride in the fact that he had always been a safe driver. In the 1940s when he drove the streetcars in downtown Los Angeles, he had received an award for safe driving, and—incredibly—in his roughly fifty years of driving the family car he had never been involved in an accident. Now he was being told it was not safe for him to get behind the wheel, and it brought an anger to the surface that was uncharacteristic of the father I knew.

And then during that afternoon chat, Dad said something I did not expect.

He leaned in. "There's something you should know," he whispered. "Your mother is having an affair."

I wanted to laugh, but I held my serious expression. Mom always got frustrated when he said outrageous things and tried to correct him, which only angered Dad. I just played along.

"Really?" I asked.

"Yes," he said emphatically.

"Who's she having an affair with?"

"With Floyd." Their pastor.

At the time, I knew it was the Alzheimer's talking and simply dismissed it. Of course Mom would not be having an affair with her minister. The notion was absurd on so many levels. But looking back on it now, I wonder if Dad's diseased mind was retrieving a distant memory from a different time and in a different context. Had he suspected something really was going on back in the fifties? Had he come across a piece of evidence back then? A note, perhaps? Maybe there were callers who would hang up the phone when he answered. Was it possible the Alzheimer's disease had unlocked suspicions he had long suppressed and they had broken through that afternoon with me?

Cindy and I arrived in Tehachapi around 5:30 a.m., with my sister close behind us. First we drove to the hospital, which was located in the heart of town. It was a very small building, more of a doctor's office than a hospital. It had a tiny parking lot, and at that hour it was virtually empty. I looked for my brother's truck and my parents' car, the one Dad drove until they took his license away. But I didn't see either vehicle. They had left. I knew what that meant.

My father was gone.

CHAPTER 13

Can I Still Do My Job?

December 19, 2012

The walk from the New York Stock Exchange to Bobby Van's Steakhouse takes maybe one minute. That's if you're in no hurry. If it's cold outside, as it was that Wednesday afternoon in late December 2012, you walk faster and it takes no time at all to make it across Broad Street, up the front steps, through the restaurant's entrance, and into the warmth of the reception area. I checked my overcoat and seated myself at the bar. Ordinarily I would order an iced tea, since it was midday and I would be on the air in a few hours. But on this day I asked for a beer. Then I waited for my lunch date.

Larry Kramer was my agent, but first he was my friend. He and I worked together at CNBC in the nineties. He worked in the legal department before he left to pursue a new career as an agent. Eventually he started his own agency, and he built up an impressive clientele of many well-known TV news personalities. We had spent a lot of time over the years discussing my professional plans for the future, and he saw it as his mission to help me carry out those plans.

Larry needed to know about my situation, and I needed to unload this burden on someone I could trust, so I e-mailed him a lunch invitation and we set a date close to Christmas, on December 19. The day before we were to get together, I texted him a heads-up, letting him know I had some news for him about a life-changing experience I had had. It was not life threatening, I assured him, and no, Cindy and I were not splitting up. But it was going to blow him away.

A few minutes after noon, a tall, athletic redhead walked through the restaurant's beveled glass doors. Before he worked in television Larry had been a tennis pro at a country club; even now, in his forties, he was a nationally ranked amateur. We shook hands and chatted about this and that as he unbuttoned his overcoat and unwound his scarf. I knew that he was thinking about my text message, but I also knew that he was not going to be the one to bring it up. It was up to me to set the agenda. I suggested we head to our table. After we were seated he ordered a diet soda and we both looked over our menus while we chatted.

The waiter brought his drink. He took a sip and set the glass down.

"So . . . ," I said, and paused.

Larry looked at me with a curious expression.

"I can't imagine," he said.

I gave him the long version, about Doug's asking me to take a DNA test, the weird initial result, and the retest. All the while I gauged Larry's expression, wondering if he would guess what was coming before I got there. But the look on his face told me he didn't have a clue. When I got to the events of October 4, his expression was one of both apprehension and curiosity.

Finally, I hit him with the punch line.

"—and my cousin informed me that my father may not have been my father."

"No!" He exhaled the word loudly and with force, like a cross-court winner.

I took a sip of my beer and let the story sink in. I knew the progression of feelings he had to be experiencing: confusion, bewilderment, shock. How should he respond? With pity? Should he laugh? He studied me, desperate for direction. I gave it to him: I smiled.

"Pretty incredible, isn't it?" I purposely affected a nonchalant attitude.

Larry's a lawyer. He thinks like a lawyer. He started peppering me with lawyerly questions.

"Are these DNA labs reputable?"

"Good question," I said. I assumed so.

"Have you told your mother yet?" No. Still waiting for the results of the second sample.

"Was your mother the type of person to have an affair?" No way.

Assuming this was true, Larry said, could I think of any time in my life when she might have tipped her hand? When she acted strange? I had thought about that, I told him, and nothing came to mind.

"Do you have any idea who your real father might be—if this is true?" No clue.

"Do you look like your siblings?" While the resemblances weren't striking, there were similarities.

When the waiter brought our food we took a break from the conversation. Talking things out with Larry was like spilling all of the pieces of a jigsaw puzzle onto a table and sorting through them. He was helping me identify the edge pieces so I could get a better sense of the parameters of what I was dealing with.

Larry agreed with Cindy and Terryll that there had to have been a mix-up with my first sample. This was just too bizarre. But if it was true, he said, I absolutely needed to tell my mother. I repeated my concern that it might do real damage to her health. This would be a terrible shock to her system, I argued. She would feel profound shame. And I didn't want it to define the final years of her life. Larry understood, but he agreed with Chuck. My mother was the only person who could answer my questions, and I should not wait too long to start asking them.

We finished our lunch and went our separate ways. I promised to let him know the moment I got the second lab result.

As I walked back across Broad Street toward the stock exchange, I thought about the other reason Larry needed to know all of this. The unspoken question between us at lunch was obvious: Was the stress of my situation going to hamper my ability to do my job? Friendship is one thing, but business is business. I was doing everything I could to maintain my energy and enthusiasm on the air, but off-camera I was still terribly shaken. What if it started to affect my performance? At this level in the TV news business, network executives do not criticize "the talent" face to face. They call their agents. If my bosses didn't like something, Larry would be the person who would get the phone call. And he needed to have answers. From this point on, I knew Larry would be watching me closely on television, concerned for the well-being of his friend but also making sure his client was still able to do his job.

CHAPTER 14

A Lesson from Family History

September 2006

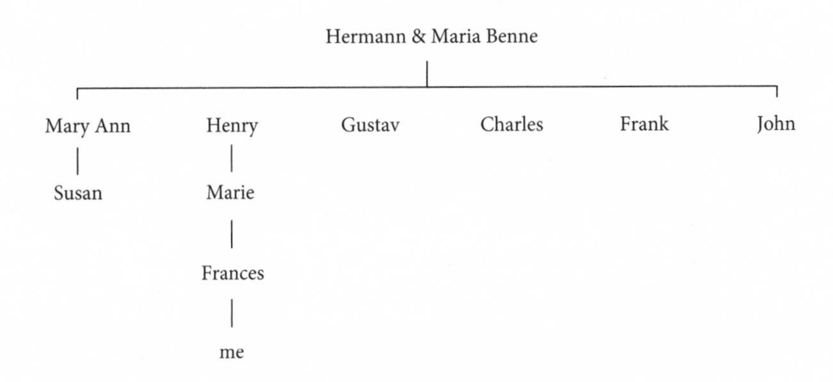

One of Larry's questions kept coming back to me: *Could I think of any time in my life when my mother might have tipped her hand?* What he was really asking was, how could my mother have been able to hide such a big secret so convincingly?

I thought I knew the answer to that. It went back to a grave I had come across in Washington, Kansas, in the fall of 2006. I was in the area doing some genealogical research and stopped at the Washington City Cemetery to pay my respects to my maternal grandmother, Marie Benne Norris, who was buried there with her parents, Henry and Bertha, and other Benne relatives.

I wiped the dirt away from Grandma's headstone, took a picture of it, and thought about all the summers I had spent in her home as a child, climbing up and down the stairs, catching fireflies in her front yard after dark, eating homemade ice cream in the front parlor.

I studied the names on the other headstones in the plot and came across one that was unfamiliar to me:

MARY ANN BENNE, 1846–1916.

I thought I knew all the Bennes. Was she someone's wife? But whose? When I got home, I called my mother and asked her who this Mary Ann was.

"Oh, that was Grandpa Henry's sister," she said, referring to my great-grandfather. There was an odd tone to her voice. I could tell she didn't want to talk about this. But I pressed her.

"She never married?" I asked.

"No." Short answer.

"How come I never heard about her before?"

"I have no idea."

It was becoming clear that there was more to this mystery woman's story, but my mother was not going to tell me what it was, which only made me more curious. I did some more research on my own until I finally uncovered the sad story of my great-aunt Mary Ann Benne.

My great-great-grandparents Hermann and Maria Benne, circa 1870

My great-great-grandparents, Hermann and Maria Benne, left Germany in the spring of 1845 on a passenger ship named the *Luntine*. They were packed below deck in steerage with 230 other immigrants from Germany and Eastern Europe, in conditions that were notoriously bad and the food often inedible. According to family lore, the Bennes had an infant with them, a son named Hermann Jr., but he did not survive the difficult journey and was buried at sea. The *Luntine* finally made port in New Orleans on June 23. The ship's manifest said Hermann was 25 and Maria was 27. From New Orleans, Hermann and Maria took a steamboat up the Mississippi River to Saint Louis, and eventually they settled on farmland in nearby Morgan County, Missouri.

A year after their arrival in America, in 1846, Maria gave birth to a daughter they named Marianna. In census records from later years she is listed as Mary Ann, and sometimes just Ann. Two years after that, in 1848, my great-grandfather Henry was born; then came sons Gustav and Charles. The Bennes lived in Missouri for ten years and then moved north to the Minnesota Territory, to a German enclave twenty-five miles southwest of Minneapolis called Shakopee. Two more sons, Frank and John, were born there.

By 1870 my great-great-grandmother Maria's health was beginning to deteriorate because of the harsh winters in the northern plains, so the Bennes moved again. In the late fall, five members of the family—Hermann, Maria, Mary Ann, Henry, Frank, and John—headed south for Kansas in covered wagons, leaving behind 20-year-old Gus and 17-year-old Charlie. It was an eventful trip. Just as they crossed the border from Nebraska into Kansas, they got caught in an early-season blizzard. Desperate for shelter and with no place to go, they were rescued by an Irish immigrant named William Holland, who had arrived in the area only a few months earlier with his wife and children. Because there were so few trees in that part of the country, Holland had built for his family the kind of crude, temporary mud house that was common in the area. He was just emerging from this dugout when he spotted the Benne wagons passing by in the storm. He knew the travelers would soon be in trouble, so he saddled his horse, caught up with them a few miles down the road, and invited them to stay with his family. The invitation was gratefully accepted. For the next three days, twelve men, women, and children were crowded into William Holland's primitive dugout while the blizzard passed through. The story was, they lived on nothing more than boiled potatoes.

Hermann eventually homesteaded 160 acres near the Hollands' farm in Union Township, Washington County, Kansas, and 23-year old-Henry took a claim on eighty acres a mile to the east. As the years went by, the Benne sons married and started their own families. Henry married a local German girl, Bertha Gravelle, and they had nine children, including my grandmother Marie. Henry's younger brother Frank moved with his wife and children to Oklahoma, and the youngest brother, John, settled with his family on land next to Hermann's farm.

Mary Ann was another story. She never married, but in 1876, the year she turned 30, she gave birth to a daughter she named Susan. Two years later Great-Grandma Maria died and was buried on the family farm.

Then things got very messy.

It is clear that Hermann was a difficult man with a strong personality. One of his grandsons would later remember him as being "headstrong" and "stubborn." And in a brief family history written by one of his granddaughters, someone had hastily scribbled a word in the margin to describe the family patriarch: "drinker."

A local researcher in Kansas who was doing some work for me in 2006 unexpectedly dug up a document in the Washington County records submitted by a lawyer representing Hermann Benne. It was dated August 18, 1879.

Your petitioner, the undersigned, respectfully represents that whereas one Ann Benne was on the 5th day of August AD 1879 adjudged by the Probate Court to be of unsound mind and incapable of managing her own affairs or taking care of herself. Furthermore the said Ann Benne has an Illegitimate Child about four years old called and named Susan Benne. And that the said child may not become a charge to the County or become a vagrant for the want of parental care, your petitioner prays your honor to appoint Hermann Benne as the Legal Guardian of the person of the said child Susan Benne. Your petitioner furthermore pledges himself to maintain and educate said child as if it were his own.

Hermann had signed the bottom of the petition with an X, and his request had been granted. He became the legal guardian of his granddaughter Susan, and then he had his daughter, Mary Ann, committed to the Washington County Poor Farm, where she spent the rest of her life—thirty-seven long years. I found her listed as a resident of the poor farm in six different census records between 1880 and 1915. One record noted she could neither read nor write. Another indicated she spoke only German. Another said she worked as a servant.

The Washington County Poor Farm in Logan, Kansas

Was Mary Ann mentally disabled? Is that why Hermann sent her away, because after Maria died he couldn't care for a disabled and dependent daughter and a young granddaughter all by himself? Or was he so ashamed of what his daughter had done that he couldn't stand to look at her? After some gentle prodding, my mother told me that her mother once said there was nothing wrong with Mary Ann Benne.

My great-grandfather Henry Benne occasionally visited his sister at the poor farm, but she never reciprocated, either because she was unable to or unwelcome. When she died in the summer of 1916 at the age of 70, Henry paid for her funeral and she was quietly buried in the family plot.

Meanwhile, Great-Great-Grandpa Hermann raised his granddaughter on the family farm. They were listed in the 1880 census as a 59-year-old widower farmer and his 4-year-old "daughter" Susie. Five years later, in the 1885 Kansas state census, the 64-year-old Hermann and 9-year-old "Sue" were still together. It was the last time either of them would be listed together in any record. Hermann died in 1893 at the age of 72, when Susie was 17. No one in the family today knows what happened to her after that. She simply vanished.

I did some digging and found a Susan Benne listed in an Omaha, Nebraska, city directory from 1923. The listing suggested that she was a waitress in a café and lived by herself in an upstairs apartment two doors away. A very small existence. Our Susan Benne would have been 47-years-old in 1923. Was this Mary Ann's daughter, a single middle-aged woman living a quiet life only a few hours from a family that didn't want to acknowledge her existence?

It is likely that no one in Omaha knew the circumstances of Susan's birth or that her mother had died a pauper on a county poor farm. But my mother knew, and as a result she understood what happened to "fallen women." Family is supposed to be about unconditional love, but what my mother learned from Mary Ann's story was that unconditional love had its limits. And I now suspected that lesson had had a great influence on her life.

CHAPTER 15

"You Will Always Be a Griffeth"

December 21, 2012

Just before Christmas I received an e-mail from my cousin Nancy: *What did you find out about your DNA test? I've been wondering about it and hope it showed different results this time around.*

Nancy and I were fourth cousins. Our great-great-grandfathers, Carlos and Ambrose Griffeth, were brothers. She was born and raised in Kansas, and after a career as a nurse she retired and moved to Florida with her husband. She was one of a handful of relatives Doug and I corresponded with around the country about our family's history. Nancy was the only one of them I confided in about my DNA issue.

I wrote back to her.

No results yet, so I'm trying to take this one step at a time, and not let my imagination get carried away too much, but that's hard to do. If my father wasn't my father, then who was??? Since my mom was a housewife at the time of my birth, I'm thinking the only people she would have come in contact with were our neighbors. I did sort of look like two brothers who lived on our block. . . . But I don't want to go there yet. (Isn't this crazy??????)

Nancy responded the next day:

This kind of thing will drive you nuts if you let it! Don't do it. I know it is hard to wait; however, wait until you get the results before you start questioning everything. Do you look anything like your brother? I don't look a thing like my sister; however, we both have the same mom and dad. The chances of your mom having an affair with your neighbor are SLIM!! Are you sure you were not adopted? When I was a kid, I thought I was adopted because I was so different from my parents and sister. However, when I got older, I was a lot like my dad. Have you ever had a lab test come back with bad results? Then they do a retest and everything is fine? I have. Look at it that way until you know something for sure. No matter what, you are a Griffeth. You were raised as a Griffeth and you will always be a Griffeth! :)

Chuck, Doug, and me in Kansas City, 2012

I e-mailed Nancy a photo of Chuck and Doug and me taken outside a barbecue restaurant during our ancestor hunt in Kansas that summer, and I attached a note:

Chuck and I aren't exactly twins (he is 16 years older than me, remember) but we share many of the same mannerisms. No way am I adopted. My mother really was pregnant, and I look exactly like her mother. I am definitely my mother's son. My brother keeps asking if it was possible our parents brought the wrong baby home. Ha ha.

My mother in an affair? That's the big issue. That's where I have driven myself nuts. It just does not compute. So we take it one step at a time.

She wrote back on Christmas Eve:

Great picture of all three of you. Your brother is laughing about the wrong baby deal because these test results aren't his. This is obviously important to you; however, remember . . . you are a Griffeth all your life. The test results don't really matter that much in the overall picture of things. I still think the [first] test results were not yours. Just be patient a little while longer. :)

MERRY CHRISTMAS!
Nancy

As it turned out, I didn't have to wait much longer.

CHAPTER 16

Results

January 3, 2013

I developed a daily ritual while I waited for my DNA test results to arrive. Each morning I logged on to the lab's website, hoping something had been posted overnight, and then I logged on again in the evening when I got home from work. December 2012 came and went. No results.

Until Thursday, January 3, 2013. It was around 6:30 in the evening. Chad and I were both home from work by then, and Carlee was home after finishing her final semester in college. Cindy announced that dinner was almost ready when I realized that I hadn't yet checked the DNA website.

"Give me a second," I said as I hurried to the study. "This won't take long."

I sat down at my desk, logged on, and quickly typed the letters and numbers that were my personal PIN code.

"Dad," Carlee called out from the kitchen. "Dinner's on the table."

"Be right there," I called back.

I got to the final step and the button that read *See Your Results*. I clicked on it, expecting to see that my sample was still being verified. Then I would log off and head to dinner. But this time there was a brief pause after I clicked—that had never happened before—and then an animated graphic as the pages of an electronic book opened up before me, and there, finally, in an elaborate two-page display, were my results. The page on the left was a description of my X chromosome, or maternal ancestry, and the page on the right was about my paternal Y chromosome.

"Dad!"

"Just a second," I said softly, almost to myself, as I intently studied the computer screen.

The page on the left showed that, as expected, my X chromosome matched Chuck's, meaning we shared the same mother. The right kid had come home from the hospital after all.

I anxiously turned my attention to the page on the right. There in large fancy letters and numbers was the scientific designation of my Y chromosome:

I-Z138

My haplogroup was indeed I, not R like Chuck and Doug's.

So that was it. Doug had been right all along. *Your father was not Uncle Charles.*

I now knew the truth for sure. My position in my family was indeed unusual. I was different, but in ways I could never have imagined. This went way beyond being a "pleasant surprise."

I did not experience a panic attack with this revelation like the one I had in October when the first DNA test result arrived. There was no ringing in my ears this time, no anger, no agitation. Only resignation. There could be no more denial. I had run out of straws to grasp. There were no more alternate scenarios with tidy explanations. Game over; I had lost.

I logged off and headed to dinner. When I walked into the kitchen, Cindy and the kids were seated at the table, the food on their plates untouched. Their conversation stopped and all three of them stared at me.

They knew.

CHAPTER 17

"Nothing Has Changed in Your Life"

January 4, 2013

The next morning Chad got up and went to work, Cindy headed to church for a volunteer project, and Carlee remained in bed sleeping off her semester. I had the house to myself. After breakfast, I climbed the stairs to our bedroom and sat down in the easy chair next to the bay window that faced west. It was a typical January morning in the Northeast. The sky was iron gray and, with no breeze to move the spindly tree branches, there was a cold, barren stillness to the landscape. Mother Nature had long ago packed it in for the winter.

I thought about an e-mail I received that morning from Cousin Nancy in Florida.

Dear Bill,

OK, so now you have the final DNA results. Please explain to me what has changed in your life. Exactly. Nothing has changed in your life.

Practically speaking, she was right. My present life remained untouched. I still had the same wife and children, the same house, same car, same job, same friends. Nothing around me had changed.

But I felt different. A curtain had been pulled back, revealing a new truth about my past. A devastating truth: I had been deceived by the people I trusted the most, my parents.

I thought back to the Christmas morning when I had figured out that there was no Santa Claus. I don't remember how old I was—maybe 8 or 9—when I ran into the living room to see what was under the tree and was thrilled to find a free-standing chalkboard with a large red bow attached to it. It was magnificent.

There was a message on the board written in white chalk:

> To Billy.
> Merry Christmas from Santa.

I recognized my mother's handwriting, and in that instant I knew the truth. Every child who grows up believing in Santa eventually figures it out, and it dawns on them that their parents have been lying to them. Then there are the awkward moments when they know that you know, there are the sly winks and smiles, and life goes on.

But *this*.

If genealogy had taught me anything, it was that when our lives are stripped to the bare walls—no job, no money, no possessions—we are left with a fundamental truth that defines us, and it's *family*. Careers and professional achievements are filed under "What We Do." It's *family* that makes us "Who We Are." Family relationships supersede all others. You may not get along with your relatives, and you may not be interested in your ancestry, but you cannot escape their influence. *Family* gave you your looks and your mannerisms, and helped shape your very identity.

During the decade of intense research I did on Griffeth family history, I stuffed six large binders with photos and notes and stories and records about dozens of individuals, nine generations in all. I may never have met them, but each person was still special to me because we shared an exclusive bond. We were family.

But now this DNA test told me that I had been pursuing a false lead. These people were not my family.

Or were they?

Cousin Nancy argued that the results didn't matter. I was still a Griffeth, she said. *You were raised as a Griffeth and you will always be a Griffeth!*

But even though my birth certificate said I was a Griffeth, a DNA test said I wasn't, at least not biologically.

My whole life, I believed that this was what my family looked like on a genealogical chart:

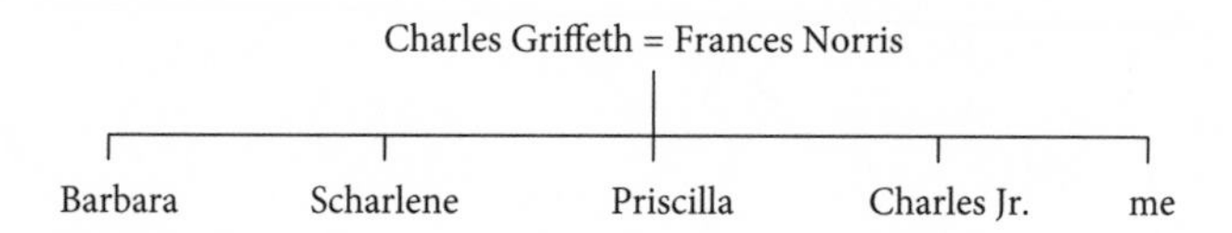

This had been my fundamental truth. I was the fifth child and second son of Charles and Frances Griffeth. They were my parents. And that fact could never be taken away from me.

But, incredibly, it was taken away. And this became my fundamental truth:

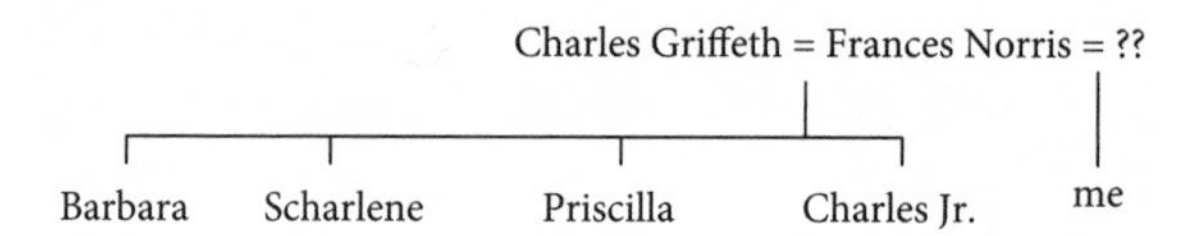

It was decision time. I could go on as if nothing had changed. I could continue to tell the world that Charles Griffeth was my father. No one would have to know. Or I could pursue the real truth, this unbelievable turn of the screw, and start asking some very uncomfortable questions.

I was torn. If I chose to learn the identity of my biological father, where would that leave my feelings toward the man who raised me? And what if the mystery man was still alive? Was there room in my life—*in my heart*—for him?

I settled more deeply into the easy chair as everything washed over me: the three unsettling months of troubling questions . . . the distressing revelations . . . the lies uncovered—*the lies!*—and the gravity and magnitude of it all.

I knew what I had to do, and I hated it. Mom's ninety-fifth birthday was coming up at the end of the month, and Cindy and I had planned a trip to California to celebrate it with her. At her age, each birthday became more precious. Who knew how many more there would be? And now there was a good chance I was going to spoil it with my alarming questions.

I laid my head on the arm of the easy chair and began to sob, quietly at first, and then I just let go. Everything I had been holding in for three months came out in a flood of tears. The last time I had cried uncontrollably like that was the morning my father died. And now it felt like he was dying all over again.

Part II

Pilate asked him, "What is truth?"

—John 18:38

CHAPTER 18

Who Is My Father?

January 2013

And so the guessing game began. Who could my biological father be? It was a bizarre, unsettling exercise. First I had to get my head around the idea that my mother had strayed. Obviously she had. I was living proof.

How did my mother meet the mystery man? My parents didn't socialize much. Both were painfully shy. They were uneasy in group situations. Idle conversation was not their thing. All of which made this so puzzling. Who in the world could have insinuated himself so intimately into my mother's life?

Was it someone she worked with? After my folks moved to the San Fernando Valley in the late 1940s, Mom had worked for the nursery, but by the time they sold their farm and moved to Reseda in 1955, she had left that job, and I was unaware of any other job she may have had. So there were no coworkers to put on the suspect list.

Church friends? They didn't attend any local church until I was five years old, so that ruled that out.

Which left our neighbors. I'd grown up on a street full of families. Virtually all of the mothers were housewives, and the fathers held a variety of professional jobs. A few, like my father, worked in the aerospace industry. And there was one man who worked in production at Universal Studios. Another was an actor who had played bit parts on various TV shows. And there was a dentist. The neighbor I liked the best lived next door. Mr. Blackwell drove a catering truck, and each day when he returned home from work in the late afternoon, I would race over as he was unloading the unsold pastries and cans of soda, and I would grab a chunk of shaved ice from the back of the truck, put it in my mouth and let it melt while I watched him work. He would ask me about my day at school, and we would chat about whatever. If I could choose one of our neighbors to be my biological father, it would have been Mr. Blackwell. I loved him. But there was no way. He had dark leathery skin and a large Roman nose. We could not have looked more different.

What about the other fathers on the block? The dentist and the actor had both had jet-black hair and an olive complexion, so they were eliminated. Mr. Universal Studios was my best friend's father, and while he was handsome, and probably very popular with the ladies, he was too young for my mother and he didn't seem like her type.

Ultimately, I narrowed the list down to two possibilities.

First there was the family across the street. I will call them the Smiths. Mr. Smith worked in aerospace like Dad did. Everyone called him Bud. I did some research and learned that his given name was Vernon. He was born in Minnesota in 1919, which made him a year younger than Mom. But he had seemed much older. In fact, he'd looked a lot like the actor William Frawley, who played Fred Mertz, the surly next-door neighbor on *I Love Lucy*. Bud Smith had the same permanent scowl and gruff manner as Frawley—not exactly the romantic type likely to woo the neighbor lady across the street.

I would have dismissed Bud outright except for one thing. The Smiths had two daughters. The younger one was my first playmate in life, and we could easily have been brother and sister. Both of us had the same fair complexion, the same blond hair, and very similar demeanors. We did everything together. We climbed trees in my backyard and chased butterflies in hers. She played ball with me, and I tolerated her tea parties. And we fought like siblings but we always made up. Eventually, as we got older, she and I grew apart when it wasn't cool for boys and girls to like each other. And then the Smiths moved away and we lost touch completely.

As unlikely as it seemed, Bud Smith could have been my biological father. The circumstantial evidence was compelling. He was right across the street and worked for the same company my father did—they sometimes even carpooled to work—all of which made it possible that he could have developed a relationship with my mother. And the fact that one of his daughters could have been my twin almost sealed the deal for me.

But Bud Smith didn't finish at the top of my list of suspects. That distinction fell to a man I will call Mr. Jones.

The Jones family lived two doors from us, on the corner. Mr. Jones was of average height and medium build, just like me. He had fair skin and blonde hair, just like me. And his first name was Bill.

In fact, I learned during my research that we shared the same initials: W. C. He was William Charles and I was William Curtis. As I mentioned, I was named for both of my grandfathers, David William Norris and Curtis Orvillo Griffeth, and I often wondered why I got Grandpa Dave's middle name instead of his first name. Was this why I wasn't named David Curtis? Did my mother name me William in a secret nod to my actual biological father?

Mr. and Mrs. Jones had two sons. The younger one was named Jimmy. He was a year younger than me, and he looked just like me: slight build, round face, fair skin, and blond hair. But Jimmy and I were never that close. He was a loner who pretty much kept to himself. Years later, after we had graduated from high school, he started dealing drugs. One day, out of the blue, Mom told me that Jimmy had been murdered during a drug deal that went bad. It was horrifying news, of course, but I always thought it was odd that she had bothered to tell me about it, since Jimmy and I were never really friends. Had she quietly been keeping tabs on the Jones family all of these years?

I told Cindy of my suspicions about Mr. Smith and Mr. Jones, and she did some of her own research. One evening when I came home from work, I found the yearbook from my senior year in high school on the kitchen table.

"I want to show you something," Cindy said as she picked it up and flipped through the pages. "I found a picture of Jimmy Jones, and he looks nothing like you."

She came to the page she was looking for and pointed to a thumbnail photo.

"See?" she said.

I studied the young man in the picture.

"That's not Jimmy Jones." I pointed to another photo two places over. "*That's* Jimmy Jones. They mixed up the names."

His hair was a little darker than I remembered, but I still saw a resemblance through the eyes and the familiar Charlie Brown roundness of his face. It was hard to believe that a few short years later, this quiet, roly-poly kid would be found dead in a giant drain pipe with a bullet in his brain.

Was Bill Jones my biological father? And if he was, how and why did he and my mother connect? Was it during the day, when Dad was at work and my brother Chuck was in school? Where did they rendezvous? Our house or theirs? And where was Mrs. Jones at those times? I don't remember if she had a job outside the home, but I do remember that the Joneses divorced when Jimmy and I were still in elementary school, and Mr. Jones moved out. Was it because Mrs. Jones found out?

I came across a photo of Bill Jones online, taken many years after I knew him. His blond hair had turned white, but otherwise he still looked like the man I remembered. His eyes and the shape of his face were similar to mine, and so was his smile. Records revealed that he passed away in 2003 and was buried next to Jimmy. Of all the men I'd known when I was a child, I was convinced that this man, who looked like me and shared my name, could be my father.

I was wrong.

CHAPTER 19

Mom's Complicated Family

August 7, 2012

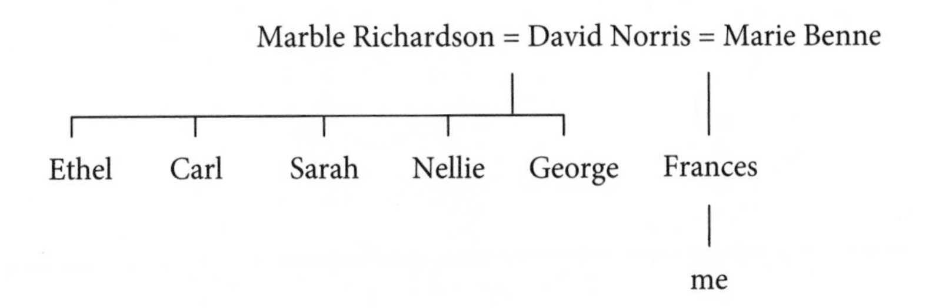

"Do you see it?"

"No. Not yet."

It was day three of our August ancestor hunt through Kansas, and we were slowly navigating a very hilly dirt road, looking for the farmhouse my mother had grown up in. I was driving our rental car with Doug seated next to me, and Cindy was in the backseat. Chuck and Terryll were following in their car. I was on my cell phone with Mom so she could give me directions to her childhood home.

"It shouldn't be far now," she said. We had been on the phone for close to thirty minutes while she guided me through the territory she knew so well. I didn't say anything, but I didn't think we were going to find what we were looking for. The old Norris farmhouse would now be more than 120 years old. Even by country standards, that was old. My grandparents sold the farm in 1930 when Grandpa Dave was 72 and unable to keep it going. And now, 82 years later, Mom insisted the house would still be standing, but I was very doubtful.

"I think we turn left here," Cindy called out as she studied the

GPS on her iPad. I turned left.

"What are you seeing?" Mom asked.

"Nothing yet," I said. "Just a lot of trees."

But once we passed the trees and came to a clearing, there, off in the distance, was the outline of a farmhouse. It couldn't be, I thought.

But it was.

"I told you!" Mom gloated as we got out of our cars and walked up the dusty driveway.

The old Norris farmhouse in Lowe Township, Kansas, where my mother grew up, 2012

(The small dark yucca plant my grandfather planted a hundred years ago can be seen to the left of the front walk.)

The house had obviously been abandoned for quite a long time. This happened a lot in the area. Old farms were purchased by people who had no interest in living on the property. Instead, they worked the land but lived elsewhere, and the farmhouses were left to decay.

Cindy and Terryll walked around taking photos, Doug wandered to the back of the property to do some exploring, and Chuck and I headed for the front of the house. I kept Mom on the line.

"Do you see the yucca plant?" she asked me.

"The what?"

"The yucca plant. It's next to the walkway in the front yard."

"What is a yucca plant doing in Kansas?" I asked. "It belongs in the desert."

"Grandpa took a trip to California in the early 1900s and brought it back with him."

"Here it is," Chuck called back. He was standing on the stone walk our grandfather had put in, and there next to it was the century-old yucca plant. Its pointy green fronds, shooting out like a starburst, definitely looked out of place in a field of overgrown switchgrass.

"Unbelievable," I said.

"I told you," Mom said again.

Chuck ventured up to the front porch, but clearly the rotting steps weren't going to hold his weight, and the front door was barely hanging on its hinges. There would be no tour of the inside. We would have to be content with peering through windows.

I asked Mom to give me a virtual tour of the house where she had spent the first twelve years of her life. She told me her parents' bedroom was downstairs, just off the living room, and hers was upstairs above the kitchen.

The kitchen. I didn't bring it up, but I thought of a story she told me long ago about an incident that occurred in that kitchen, when she got her own stunning family surprise. She was only 7 or 8 years old when she arrived home from school one afternoon to find her father sitting in the kitchen with a man she did not recognize.

"Meet your brother!" Grandpa said enthusiastically as she walked through the door.

My maternal grandfather, Dave Norris, was a complicated man who had lived a difficult life. He'd inherited very different traits from each of his parents. He shared the wandering tendencies of his free-spirited father, George, and the strict moral code of his domineering mother, Sarah.

My grandfather David William Norris, circa 1880

Dave was the third of eight children, born in 1858 in New Boston, Illinois. New Boston was a small shipping port on the Mississippi River laid out in 1834 by a 25-year-old surveyor named Abraham Lincoln. Dave fondly remembered the years of his youth in New Boston, especially the summer afternoons when he and his siblings walked to the riverbank and picked wild onions, which they ate for lunch with the sauerkraut their mother kept in barrels in the root cellar. After the Civil War, the Norris family moved west to Saunders County, Nebraska, just south of Omaha.

When gold was discovered in the Black Hills of the Dakota Territory in 1876, 18-year-old Dave signed up to lead wagon trains of fortune hunters from Nebraska into the rugged landscape that was sacred ground to the Lakota Sioux. He spent one summer in the lawless mining camp of Deadwood, where he was exposed to all kinds of scandalous behavior: gambling, drinking, street shoot-outs, and—most memorably for him—saloon girls in bright red dresses who enthusiastically took their clients by the hand and led them upstairs.

Clearly he was out of his element in such a place. Like his mother, Dave was a devout, conservative Christian. His mother had taught him to read using the Bible, and—like her—he could recite chapter and verse. He was also highly judgmental, condemning the use of alcohol and all leisure activities on Sunday.

He did not stay in the Black Hills for very long. One day one of the saloon girls said to him, "You don't belong here, boy. You should go home." And so he did, but he never forgot his experiences in that Gomorrah. My mother often said her father never allowed her to wear red because it reminded him of the working girls in Deadwood.

In June 1882, Dave married a neighbor girl, Thalia Marble Richardson. Marble, as she was called, had deep Yankee roots extending back to early colonial Maine and New Hampshire. Dave and Marble had five children, Ethel, Carl, Sarah, Nellie, and George. My grandfather's wandering spirit took his family to different parts of Nebraska and Missouri before they finally settled for good in the late 1890s on the farm in Washington County, Kansas, where they raised their family.

The Norris children all went to school in the one-room Lowe Center schoolhouse situated on the northeast corner of the Norris property, and the young women who taught there roomed with the family. In the fall of 1910, 19-year-old Marie Benne was hired to teach at Lowe Center. She was a local girl whose family farm was located only a few miles east of the school. At that time, the Norris household included the three younger children: 17-year-old Sarah, 14-year-old Nellie, and 12-year-old George.

On June 1, 1913, just as young Marie's third year at Lowe Center was coming to an end, the course of the Norris family's life was tragically altered when Marble died of cancer at the age of 49. The Norris children were devastated by the loss of their beloved mother. And their sorrow was compounded when, in their eyes, they also lost their father a short time later. Incredibly, only one year after their mother's death, on June 8, 1914, Dave Norris and Marie Benne left the farmhouse without telling anyone what they were doing and drove sixteen miles north, across the state border, to Fairbury, Nebraska, where they were quietly married by a justice of the peace. He was 56 and she was 22.

I have never discussed my grandparents' courtship with my mother, so I have no idea what it was like or how it began. I'm left to imagine what might have occurred during the brief, sorrow-filled months between Marble's death and Dave and Marie's wedding. Was there a first knowing glance, a comforting touch, a quiet word whispered?

My grandparents Dave and Marie Norris
on their wedding day, June 8, 1914

I have to believe that my grandfather was profoundly sad and lonely after losing his wife of thirty-one years, whom he had known since they were teenagers. And he was well past his prime, so he must have realized that finding a new companion would be a challenge. Farm life was isolating, and social gatherings were rare. But here was this young teacher living under his roof, and she was certainly available. The teaching contract Marie had signed when she took the position in Lowe Center forbade her from "keeping company with men." There was to be "no loitering downtown in ice cream stores," it specified, and she was required to "be home between the hours of 8:00 pm and 6:00 am unless in attendance at a school function."

My guess is that theirs was a courtship of convenience. My grandfather was looking for companionship and my grandmother was looking for security. I have no idea if love was involved. Maybe that came later.

The Norris and Benne families clearly were scandalized by the turn of events. Marie's mother, my great-grandmother Bertha Benne, who was seven years younger than her new son-in-law, dismissed him as an "old fool." And my grandfather Dave's 20-year-old daughter Sarah, who was only two years younger than her new stepmother, immediately left home and moved in with her sister Ethel, who lived with her husband on a nearby farm.

Seven months after Dave and Marie were married, the 1915 Kansas state census was taken. The order of persons in their household listing was telling:

Norris, David 56
Norris, George 16
Norris, Marie 23
Norris, Nellie 18

Instead of putting Mrs. Norris second, which was customary in census records, she was listed third, after her 16-year-old stepson, George, and ahead of 18-year-old stepdaughter, Nellie, making it appear as though the middle-aged Dave Norris lived with his three children. Was there some misunderstanding on the part of the census taker, or was this how the family was presented to him by my embarrassed grandparents?

Either way, I'm uncomfortable just looking at the record. It had to have been awkward for everyone to undertake—and accept—new roles so soon after Marble Norris's death, especially for Nellie and George, whose former schoolteacher—and near contemporary—was now sleeping in the same bed in which their mother had died less than two years earlier.

This was the household my mother was born into.

On January 31, 1918, during a heavy snowstorm, Grandma Marie gave birth to her only child. Marie's younger brother, Erwin, who helped out on the farm, fetched their mother, my Great-Grandma Bertha, on horseback. Slowly and deliberately they made their way through the blizzard's growing mounds of windswept snow so Bertha could attend to the birth of her first grandchild. For my grandfather, the event had to have been bittersweet. His sixth child was born in the same room, and in the same bed, in which his first wife had passed away. And he named his new daughter after his older brother, Francis, who was killed as a young boy in a tragic shooting accident that haunted Grandpa Dave the rest of his life. My poor mother. The joy that her birth should have brought the family was in many ways overshadowed by death.

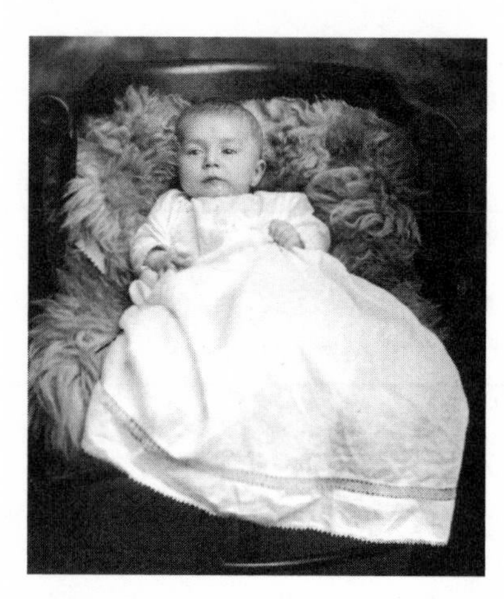

My mother, Frances Norris, as a baby, 1918

The elder Norris children essentially abandoned their father because of his second marriage, so my mother grew up as an only child, having no idea that her father had been married before—until the afternoon she came home from school and found her father sitting in the kitchen with the man he introduced as her half-brother George. Suddenly she learned she had five half siblings, and she came to realize that her bedroom had once belonged to them. How was a young child supposed to respond to such bewildering news?

Mom told me there had always been a framed photograph on a shelf in the guest bedroom, an image of her father standing next to a woman she didn't recognize. She had seen it every day but never thought to ask who the woman was. Now she knew. The woman was the first Mrs. David Norris.

It took several years for my mother to comprehend the level of animosity her half siblings had felt toward her mother when her parents were married, and the cool reception they had given her own birth. My heart always ached for her when she discussed this part of her life. She was just a little girl caught in the aftermath of what was for them an agonizing tragedy.

Mom said she was sure her father loved her, but she didn't recall receiving much affection from him. She claimed that he never held her in his lap when she was a child. If that is true, my grandfather must have been a sad and lonely man. First he lost his wife, and then, when he quickly married a new young wife, his children turned against him. I suspect he was also burdened by a deep-seated sense of guilt, which he inherited from his mother. He knew she would never have approved of the arrangement in which he now found himself, married to a much-younger woman who had been rooming in the house when his first wife died, and with a noisy, free-spirited child whom he merely tolerated in his old age.

Marie and Dave Norris at their home in Washington, Kansas, circa 1935

As it turned out, Grandpa Dave's rebound marriage to Marie lasted thirty-two years, one year longer than his union with Marble. When my grandfather died in the spring of 1946 at the age of 88, he was buried, as he had wished, beside his first wife. I don't know if that bothered my grandmother. I never asked. But I do know we never visited his grave while she was alive.

In 1930, when Grandpa Dave turned 72, he realized he could not adequately work the farm anymore, so my grandparents sold the property and moved twenty miles east to the town of Washington, Kansas. It was there that 14-year-old Frances eventually caught the eye of a high school classmate, "Chick" Griffeth, who was then 17. Mom told me she loved going to Washington High School football and basketball games and watching Dad play, and she was always in the audience when he sang bass in a quartet that performed in school productions.

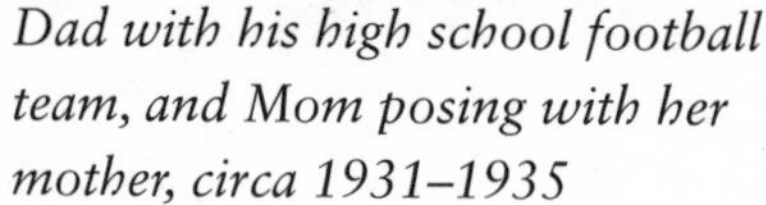

Dad with his high school football team, and Mom posing with her mother, circa 1931–1935

They became sweethearts, and they shared the same rebellious streak that had woven its way through generations of both of their families. That was never in more evidence than on the hot afternoon of June 28, 1935, a few weeks after Mom graduated from Washington High, when she put on her best dress, scribbled a note to her parents explaining what she was doing, and walked three blocks to the town square, where Dad was waiting for her. They were married in a brief ceremony at the county courthouse, in precisely the same way her parents had been united twenty-one years earlier.

My mother, the restless child of a restless man, had found her soul mate. My parents' adventure in life together, which would last fifty-two years, had begun.

CHAPTER 20

"I Want to Be Your Mother"

January 25, 2013

We were all gathered in my mother's living room. Mom was seated in her big easy chair, Cindy was on the sofa next to her, and Chuck and I were standing in front of her.

"Mom," I said gently, "Chuck and I have discovered that we have different fathers. We know that Dad was Chuck's father, but he wasn't mine. Who was my father?"

The scene ended there. Every single time. I had been playing it in my head over and over for days, rehearsing a moment I was reluctant to experience but knew was inevitable. And it always ended before Mom could answer because I had no idea how she was going to react. In the best-case scenario, she would be relieved that we finally knew the truth and she didn't have to lie anymore. The worst-case scenario was not pretty. I pictured her burying her face in her hands and wailing, and through her tears telling us to go away, that she couldn't face any of us anymore. Then she would spend the rest of her life in seclusion, ashamed and humiliated.

I did not want that to happen. I wouldn't be able to forgive myself if my questions caused her great harm. But at the same time, asking her directly was the only way I was ever going to learn the truth. Someday, when Mom died, the secret would go with her, and then I would never know what had happened. And I had to know. So the question had to be asked.

It occurred to me, as I repeated these scenarios in my head, that I should not just walk into her apartment and hit her cold with all of this. The shock might be too great for her. I decided that I should warn her ahead of time. It was only fair. So two days before we were scheduled to fly to California for her birthday celebration, I called my mom.

"I can't wait to see you," she said.

She always had a calendar hanging on the wall in her kitchen, and without seeing it I knew she had drawn a big red circle around the date of our arrival.

"Listen, Mom," I said, "There's something I'm going to want to discuss with you while we're out there."

"Okay. What's that?"

"Well, as part of my genealogical research I took a DNA test last fall. And, well, I got a weird result."

Silence.

I waited. Then I heard the soft sound of sobbing.

I panicked.

"It's no big deal!" I said. "You're still my mother." It was the first thing that came into my head. My attempt to make a joke and keep things light.

"I want to be your mother," she said earnestly through her sniffles. That sentence still haunts me. What did she mean?

I want to be your mother.

Just like that, my worst nightmare was coming true. I hadn't even told her what my weird DNA test result had revealed, but her response made it clear that she knew it wasn't good. This was precisely what I had wanted to avoid. She was all alone in her apartment, I had called with news that obviously unsettled her, and now she was going to be left to deal with it all by herself. *What have I done?* I thought. I desperately wanted to take it all back.

"Don't worry," I said. "We will sort it all out. Everything will be fine." I knew I didn't sound very convincing, but I badly wanted to get our conversation back into some sort of comfort zone. Clearly, though, that was impossible. The damage was done. There was no way we could go back to small talk, and I did not want the DNA conversation to go any further on the phone, so I hastily said how excited we were to see her and she said the same thing and then we hung up.

Cindy looked at me, her eyes wide with curiosity and concern.

"Holy shit," I said.

What had I done, indeed?

CHAPTER 21

"Let's Talk about My DNA Issue"

January 27, 2013

I am a comfortable flyer, but I do have my limits. I can only take a maximum of seven hours at a time on an airplane. That's enough to get me from the east coast of the United States to most of the major European capitals. I can't imagine being cooped up for twelve or sixteen hours at a stretch, which is largely why I have never been to Asia or Australia. The flight from the East Coast to West Coast of the United States is bad enough at roughly six hours. By the time we're over the Rockies, I'm ready to land.

But on the Sunday when Cindy and I flew to California to celebrate Mom's ninety-fifth birthday, I was in no hurry to get there. Our flight could have stayed in the air all day and it would have been fine with me. I knew that when we arrived at Burbank Airport, we would roll our suitcases out of the terminal, throw our bags in the trunk of our rental car, and head north for the hour-long drive to Mom's apartment. What I didn't know was what would happen after that, and it terrified me.

A book I'd read about coping with anxiety warned against constant rumination; that is, thinking repeatedly about a problem without working it through to a possible solution. But that was exactly what I did on the flight. All I could think about was the encounter with my mother coming up in a few hours. I pictured the scene in her apartment and the moment I asked her to explain my DNA results. I replayed our phone call from two days before and felt the panic all over again when I heard her sniffles and she said, "I want to be your mother." Over and over.

For four months I had gradually grown accustomed to the idea that my father might not be my father. And except for a very few close friends and relatives, I had kept the news to myself. I had the power to leave it alone if I chose to and move on without telling anyone else. There was a certain comfort in that. I hate drama, and I avoid conflict at all costs. I hadn't asked for this upsetting revelation. It had presented itself without invitation. But as much as I might want to, I knew I couldn't ignore it. I was going to have to deal with this, and it wasn't going to be easy. Once I posed the question to my mother, the genie would be out of the bottle. My relationship with Mom might change forever, and I might learn new information that would reshape my identity. I really did not want to do this, but it was too late. The ball was in motion.

We landed, and the movie in my head finally began to play out for real. We picked up the rental car, threw our stuff in the trunk, and headed north.

My mother had voluntarily moved to an assisted-living apartment complex in the fall of 2006, a few months before her eighty-ninth birthday. She was tired of living alone, she said, and to her credit, she knew that at her age she probably shouldn't be driving a car. Her apartment was now roughly forty-five minutes from my brother's ranch, close enough that he could help her when she needed him, and far enough away that she could remain independent. Just the way she liked it.

We pulled into the parking lot, signed the register at the front desk, and walked to her apartment at the end of a long hallway. Cindy took my hand as we walked, offering her silent reassurance. I tried to ignore the pounding in my chest and the dryness of my mouth. I was just going through the motions.

We knocked on the door, and a tiny voice called out, "Come in!" She was just rising from her easy chair as we opened the door. Her outfit was all about Valentine's Day, which was a couple of weeks away: bright red top, cream-colored pants, and a necklace of red and white beads. Her expression, though, was anything but festive.

Ordinarily when we arrived, there were enthusiastic hugs and kisses and we spoke all at once. Not this time. This time there was a tension in the air. I certainly was feeling anxious, and I sensed that she was feeling—what? Fear? Dread? Or was I just projecting my own emotions?

We hugged quietly, almost solemnly, and Mom said something about how it had been so long since our last visit. We commented on her outfit and made a fuss over her cat and the jigsaw puzzle she was working on. I surveyed her living room. She had crammed in as much of her life as she could. A bookcase Dad built was in the corner. Her TV butted up against the bookcase. Next to that was a small antique desk Cindy and I had given my parents years ago as an anniversary present. Next to that was a filing cabinet. And next to that was a large butcher-block table with a fish tank on top.

Crammed, but cozy.

On the wall above her television she had created a shrine of family photos. Dad was in the middle and their five children circled him like the hands of a clock. Barbara was at high noon, Scharlene at two o'clock, Priscilla at four o'clock, Chuck at eight, and I was at ten.

The scene with my mom began to play out just the way I had pictured it. Mom sat back down in her recliner, Cindy picked a spot on the sofa next to her, and I took a chair from the kitchen table and positioned it directly in front of my mother so that I could look her in the eye. On the end table next to Mom I saw the Bible Dad gave her a few years before he died. Next to it was the daily devotional book I had sent her for Christmas. It was only a month old, but it was already dog-eared.

And so we began. We talked about my sister Priscilla, who was back in the hospital battling a variety of ailments. We looked at Christmas cards Mom had received from several relatives. And we brought her up to date on what Chad and Carlee had been up to. We talked and talked, as if our troubling phone conversation two days earlier had never happened. A couple of times I glanced at Cindy and she gave me a sympathetic look. I took deep breaths to steady myself, and I noticed that Mom continually wrung her hands and bounced her feet nervously. But we just kept on talking.

Finally there was a lull in the conversation, and I saw my opportunity.

"Okay," I said, "let's talk about this DNA thing."

She looked down at her hands.

"Oh," she said with a sorrowful voice, "I'm so afraid of what you've found."

My heart was pounding but I pressed on. I leaned in, and in a calm and reassuring tone, almost a whisper, I told her about the DNA website and the test I had taken, ostensibly to help me find Griffeth cousins I didn't know about. (I purposely left Doug out of the narrative because I didn't want her to blame him for all of this.) When the test came back, I said, I didn't match any Griffeths. I went on to explain about Chuck's test and his results, and about the results of my second test.

She listened quietly and remained focused on her hands.

"What the tests told us," I said, "is that Chuck and I have the same mother—that would be you—but we have different fathers."

She looked up from her hands.

"Okay," she said in a surprisingly strong voice. "I made a mistake years ago when I was younger." Clearly she had been thinking about this since our phone call, and she had practiced her explanation.

I made a mistake when I was younger.

Instinctively, I put my hand up.

"Let me stop you right there," I said. "I'm glad you made that mistake, because if you hadn't, I wouldn't be here." I was anxious for her to know that there was a safety net of love below, ready to catch her.

She continued with her prepared explanation.

"It was with a man I worked for."

"At the nursery?" I asked.

"No. He ran a construction company with his brother. I worked for them for two years after we moved to Reseda."

This was news to me. I had never heard about any job at a construction company. How had I missed that?

"What was his name?" I asked.

She gave us his name. For reasons that will become clear later, I'm going to use a pseudonym and call him "Gene Wyman." (I do have his genes, and he was, after all, my "Y man.")

Bingo, I thought. I remembered seeing a man with that surname at the top of a list of people who matched me on the DNA website, meaning he and I were closely related.

"What was the brother's name?" I asked.

She told us.

"Was Gene married?"

"Yes. And his brother told me it was his second marriage."

"How old was Gene?"

"I don't know."

"Where was he born?"

"I have no idea."

As we talked it out, I suddenly felt something I had not expected: relief. I was getting a first glimpse of my world as it really was. It was like Dorothy Gale opening the door of her farmhouse after the tornado in *The Wizard of Oz* and having the world turn from black and white to color. I was now seeing the true colors of my past.

Mom wasn't finished. She asked if I remembered a Catholic church near our home called Saint Catherine of Siena.

I did. My best friend who had lived a few doors from us, the son of Mr. Universal Studios, had attended that church. Where was this going?

"Mr. Wyman's company was doing work there, and I was supposed to deliver some papers to him while he was overseeing the construction. I made the delivery, and that's when it happened."

I was so stunned I couldn't respond. That's when it happened? I was conceived on the grounds of a Catholic church. Did I really need to know this? I wanted to laugh out loud, but the solemn expression on my mother's face kept me in check. And I didn't dare look at Cindy.

"Did Dad know?" I asked.

"No," she said. "And I didn't really know myself until just now."

"But you must have had your suspicions," I said.

"No, I didn't. I really didn't. It never occurred to me until you called the other evening."

Was my mother that naive? When she discovered she was pregnant with me, it never occurred to her that the father could be the other man she had had sex with? At the Catholic church? More likely, she was just in complete denial. Either way, it would explain why I was unable to conjure any suspicious memories from my childhood. Apparently there weren't any.

I had more questions and was ready to continue our conversation, but Mom abruptly moved on to other topics.

"While you're here," she said, "I need you to move my microwave oven. I don't like it where it is."

Just like that, the DNA conversation was over. My mother had always had a remarkable ability to compartmentalize her feelings. She called it German discipline. Whatever it was, I didn't inherit it. I have never been good at hiding what I'm thinking when something is troubling me. And I guarantee that if I had just confessed something so deeply personal, it would be impossible for me to turn my attention so suddenly to a microwave oven. But that's what she did, and so we moved on.

We devoted the next few days to running errands and seeing sights and eating out, all of which was a real treat for Mom. She loved just being out and about. She and Cindy did most of the talking, carrying on a running dialogue about relatives and doctor visits and apartment gossip. I did not say much, and I don't know if my mother noticed me staring off into space for prolonged periods; if she did, she never asked what I was thinking about. We had reached an odd stalemate.

Each evening when Cindy and I returned to our hotel room, we went online to see what we could find out about this man Gene Wyman, which wasn't much. Mom had given us only three tidbits to go on. We knew his name, we knew his brother's name, and we knew that Gene was on his second marriage when Mom worked for him. That was it. We had no birth date, no birthplace, no information about children, and—most important—no indication of whether he was still alive.

Nevertheless, one evening we had a breakthrough. We found an old, fuzzy, black-and-white photograph from the 1940s or '50s in a random online archive. It showed a group of men dressed in suits. They were members of a builders' organization, and the caption said Gene Wyman was second from left. Given the quality of the photo, it was difficult to clearly make out his features, but I could still see a resemblance. The high forehead, the shape of the face, and the smile all looked familiar. It was surreal to see a stranger who looked more like me than my own father ever did.

Cindy continued to dig, but the photo was all I needed for the time being. I was still trying to process my mother's confession, and now I had a name and a photo. That was enough.

On January 31 Mom turned 95. My late sister Scharlene's stepdaughter, April, and April's daughter, Selena, joined us for the birthday celebration. April and I had grown up together. She was two years older than me, and even though we only saw each other occasionally, we had remained very close. Should I tell her, I wondered? She certainly deserved to know the truth.

I decided not to say anything, for two reasons. First, it was Mom's birthday and I didn't want to risk disrupting the festivities by taking April aside and whispering this news to her. Who knew how she would respond? Second, and maybe most important, April revered my mother. Mom was the only grandmother she had ever known. And my mother thought the world of April. My fear was that bringing this truth out into the open could irreparably damage their relationship. And neither of them deserved to have that happen.

The five of us all piled into the SUV Cindy and I had rented and drove to Chuck's ranch. Mom rode shotgun with me in the front, and Cindy sat in the back with April and Selena. We chatted and told funny stories and laughed, the way we always did. Mom was obviously enjoying herself.

On the way, we stopped at a local market to pick up a birthday cake. Mom and I remained in the car while the others went in. We just looked out the window for a while, taking in the view. It was a typical winter day in the desert. The sun was bright and the air dry and cool. We sat in silence until I couldn't take it any longer.

"Cindy and I have done a little research in the last few days," I said, "and we found a photograph of my—of Mr. Wyman. Would you like to see it?"

Mom slowly turned and looked at me, wearing an expression I had never seen before. Her eyes were dead. Spooky dead.

"No," she said flatly.

She was shutting me down.

I realized it had been a mistake to even bring it up that afternoon. It was, after all, her birthday. But we were flying out the next day, and I knew that that moment in the car was going to be our last chance during the trip to discuss Gene Wyman face to face. I couldn't resist, but I should have.

I dropped it. No more words were spoken. Our awkward silence dragged on until Cindy, April, and Selena returned, laughing and buzzing, with the festive birthday cake.

CHAPTER 22

Mistake

February 3, 2013

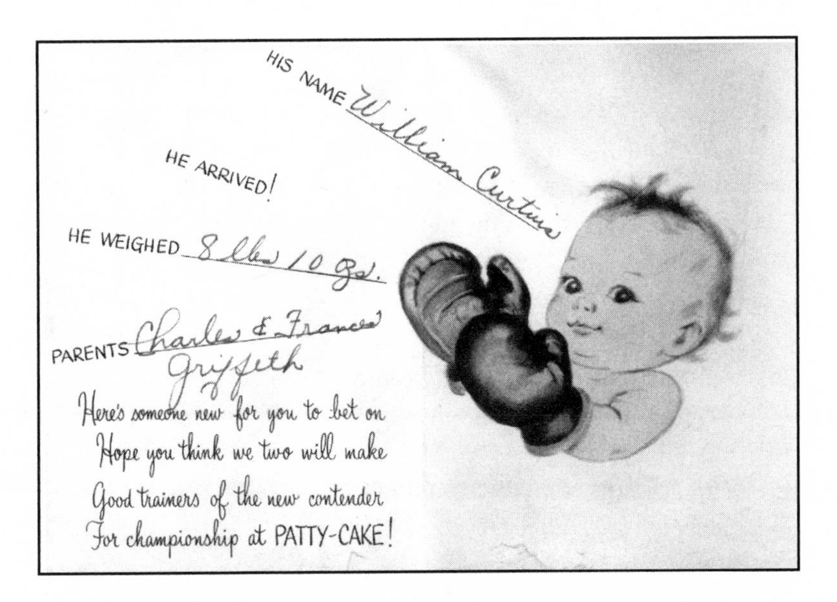

On our flight back to the East Coast, and for several days after, I replayed the conversation with my mother, over and over.

I made a mistake. . . .

It was a man I worked for . . .

Saint Catherine of Siena . . .

And that's when it happened. . . .

I made a mistake . . .

that's when it happened . . .

it happened . . .

mistake . . .

And I kept thinking *I am the product of a moment of illicit passion, an impromptu encounter between a boss and his employee on the grounds of a Catholic church.*

This was going to take some getting used to.

I wanted to know more. A lot more. But I had failed to get much information from Mom. The irony was not lost on me that even though my job as a TV anchor sometimes entailed asking the tough questions in order to get the story, I had failed to get much of anything during what was arguably the most important interview of my life. But this was my mother, I rationalized, and we were discussing a delicate matter. So I went easy on her. I admit it. She said she didn't know anything beyond the few tidbits she had revealed about Gene Wyman, but I wasn't sure I believed her. My mother had a very good memory. She could still recite the address of every house she and Dad had ever lived in. So I was a little surprised that she wasn't able to offer more information about a man who had clearly played a significant part in her life, if only for a brief period. She was either fibbing to cover her embarrassment, or—more likely—she simply never got around to asking her boss about his life. My mother wasn't one for idle chitchat.

And then it happened . . .

But how in the world *had* it happened? Was she a willing participant? Did he take advantage of her, or worse? Was I the result of a workplace rape? Could I bring myself to ask my mother such a troubling question? And if I could, would she be honest? Knowing her, she would claim she was a willing participant just to spare my feelings and to protect me from such an ugly truth. She did say, "I made a mistake," which suggested that she was accepting some of the responsibility.

It was much later that I realized something distinctive about our conversation that day. Mom had been wearing *red,* the color her father had never allowed his daughters to wear because, to him, it represented the promiscuous working girls he had encountered in Deadwood in the 1870s. I was probably overthinking this, but I couldn't get over how she had chosen to wear red that day, Was she unconsciously admitting her guilt? Maybe it was nothing more than an early Valentine's Day outfit, but I wasn't so sure.

Saint Catherine of Siena . . .

The Catholic church! The church where my closest childhood friend was baptized, where he had his First Communion, where he went to catechism. When we were in elementary school, once a week after school he and his brothers, all of them dressed in their white shirts and dark pants, had walked around the corner to that church and sat in classrooms where they were taught church doctrine. Classrooms, it turned out, that were built by my biological father. And where, apparently, I was conceived.

I tried again and again to imagine the events at Saint Catherine on the day it happened. What date would it have been? A conception calculator I found online told me that the most probable date, counting back from my birth date, was November 14, 1955, a Monday. An online almanac told me it had been a chilly 65 degrees in LA that day, and it had rained, almost three quarters of an inch.

I pictured the church. It was a landmark in our town. We passed it countless times over the years, going to and from our own Methodist church. I drove by it on my way to my college classes. It was next door to the grocery store where my mother did her shopping.

I imagined Gene Wyman pulling in at the church entrance that rainy Monday morning. Because of the weather, there were probably no workmen around, so he may have been alone. At some point he called his office and Mom answered. That was her job. She was the office manager.

Fran, could you bring me some paperwork I need? he asked. And so she did, driving the six miles from the company office in Van Nuys to the construction site in Reseda. Did he really need the paperwork, or was it a ploy on his part? Or maybe it was a code phrase they used. *Bring me the paperwork,* he would say, but she would know what he really meant. I will probably never know the answer, and it really doesn't matter. It's none of my business. I know how I got here, I just don't know why, and I guess I can live with that. What I do know is, while a chilly rain was coming down outside on that Monday in November 1955, something happened between my mother and her boss at that Catholic church.

Mistake . . .

I kept coming back to that word she used. It stuck in me like a thorn.

Mom said, "I made a mistake."

And? Was there more to her confession? Maybe something like, ". . . but I'm glad I made it"?

No, she didn't say that. That was missing from our conversation that Sunday afternoon in her apartment. She didn't say, "I made a mistake, but I'm glad I did."

I was the one who said it. I said, "I'm glad you made that mistake, because if you hadn't, I wouldn't be here."

And she didn't respond. She did not say, "I agree" or "I'm so glad you feel that way, because I do, too."

It took me a long time to put my finger on exactly what bothered me most about our conversation that day. Certainly I was troubled by the fact that my mother had strayed from her marriage. But I had had months to think about that before I confronted her.

This is what really bothered me: my mother said, "I made a mistake." And what I heard was: "I wish it—*you*—hadn't happened."

Learning that Charles Griffeth was not my father was bad enough. It had left me in a fragile emotional state. But I could not stop thinking that my mother regretted the indiscretion that led to my birth. She could not get past the act itself, *the sin,* and accept that the end—*her son*—justified the means.

I was being irrational. Of course my mother loved me. Of course she was glad that I was born. But why hadn't she said so? I knew the answer. When she confessed her sin—*her mistake*—that afternoon, she wasn't talking to Cindy and me. She was talking past us to Dad, and to her father, and to her mother, and to her God. For the first time, she was openly acknowledging something that had been buried deep inside her for more than half a century. She had betrayed the trust of people she loved, and she had had to live with that terrible secret for a very long time. But by characterizing it simply as a mistake, she was somehow diminishing its significance.

I e-mailed Cousin Nancy and poured my heart out to her, and she responded with a pep talk.

I want you to think about this carefully. Nothing in your life will change unless you want it to change. Keep that in mind as you go forward. You had nothing to do with anything that happened; therefore, you have no burden to carry. You only have additional information. It's Doug's fault that you had the DNA test to begin with! But be thankful you did it. Otherwise, you could have found this out later in your life, after your mom was gone. Then you would have had a major problem trying to find out what happened. At least this way, you know for certain how you came to be. Now you will be able to stop worrying about this and move on. Your father was your father. . . . The other guy was the sperm donor, nothing more, nothing less.

Nancy meant well. I knew she truly believed what she wrote. Nothing had to change in my life if I didn't want it to. But I wasn't able to believe it. Not yet. The wound was still too fresh, the confusion and heartache still too raw. Maybe in time.

I did laugh, though, about her dismissal of Gene Wyman as a mere sperm donor. I had been wrestling with how to refer to him. Should I call him my father? What about Charles Griffeth? It was all so confounding.

I also alerted Doug to what I had learned from my mom, and I smiled when I got his response. He was his usual pragmatic self:

Dear cousin (even if we have to go back to Adam & Eve),

Frankly, it's only fair, in my opinion, that the truth be known, as it not only affects you, but also your children. If you didn't try to get the information now, Chad and/or Carlee might choose to have their DNA analyzed, and they would confront the same anomaly! Better nip it in the bud now, as rough as it is.

Courage, my friend. That's a tough one! But I think the worst is over now.

Wow. What a story.

What a story indeed.

CHAPTER 23

Doug's Family Secret

February 8, 2013

Near disaster: during an otherwise routine e-mail exchange with Doug late one Friday evening, he casually dropped a bomb.

Forgive the impertinence of going forward with this, but I have been in e-mail contact with a Wyman gentleman who is a "0" genetic distance from you.

I had given Doug access to my account on the DNA site so he could help me understand the science. But I had not counted on anything like this.

I knew exactly whom he was referring to in his message. I had seen this "Wyman gentleman" at the top of the website's list of people who had DNA that matched mine. He and I matched on all sixty-seven of the genetic markers I had tested, meaning we were close relatives. But it was unclear exactly how we were related, so Doug had reached out to him to see if he could find out.

He has carried on a very active e-mail correspondence with his mother in an attempt to discover who your biological father is. . . . They have forwarded a photo of a Wyman who is very likely your biological grandfather, although they are not aware of any [photos] of your actual father.

I panicked. This was most definitely not how I wanted to contact the Wyman family.

I immediately logged on to the DNA lab's website and changed my password. Doug would no longer have access. And then I sent him a message demanding that he cease all contact with the Wyman family. Doug wrote back, apologizing for his "misstep," and he ended all correspondence with them. I don't know exactly what he told this Mr. Wyman about me, but we never heard from him again, and to this day I do not know how we are related.

As angry as I was with my cousin, I understood why Doug had done what he did. First of all, he felt responsible for setting this whole dramatic episode in motion. The DNA test had been his idea. But I also knew there was another reason, a much more personal reason that had to do with a secret uncovered long ago in his own family.

Uncle Dale, Aunt Opal, Mom, and Dad, circa 1952

Doug's father and mother, my Uncle Dale and Aunt Opal, were like a second set of parents to me. Dale was three years older than Dad, and although they looked a lot alike, there were differences. Dad was big and playful and athletic. Dale was shorter and slim and studious. In social settings, Dad was content to sit quietly and let others speak, but Dale was a born raconteur who loved to tell stories and jokes. I can picture many a family gathering when he held court, spinning yarn after yarn. Doug said his father would have made a great college professor, instead of a bus driver, and I agree.

My favorite relative, though, was my beloved Aunt Opal. Opal was truly my second mother. And what a character! She lived life out loud. Unlike my mother, who rarely said what she was really thinking, Opal spoke her mind—and how. She would lean toward you, squint her eyes, and point a finger, with a "Let me tell you, Buster" kind of attitude. But she also loved to laugh, and she had the greatest laugh. It was a cackle, really, but a cheerful, contagious cackle. When she laughed her eyes twinkled and her body rocked, and you couldn't help but laugh with her.

Opal came from humble beginnings. She was born in 1914 in Enid, Oklahoma, the youngest of twelve children. Both of her parents died during the Spanish influenza pandemic, leaving her orphaned at the age of six. As Opal's mother lay dying, she called her older daughters to her bedside and instructed them to watch over their little sister, which they did. After her mother's death, Opal was passed from sister to sister. By 1930, when she was sixteen, she was in Washington, Kansas, working as a live-in domestic for parents who thought so much of her they named their youngest child Opal.

In December 1931, she married Uncle Dale. He was 19 and she was 17. Almost nine months to the day later, their first child—my cousin Donna—was born. Three more children followed in the next ten years.

By the time I came along, all of my siblings and all of Dale and Opal's children were grown and out of the house. So I had the four adults all to myself. They did everything together, and I tagged along. Monday night was bowling night, and Saturday night was for playing cards. One week it would be at our house, and the next at theirs.

When we went to their house, I made a beeline from the front door to the kitchen and the drawer where Aunt Opal always kept a bag of Mother's Iced Raisin Cookies. Man, did I love those cookies. Years later, after Cindy and I moved to the East Coast, I had my mother send me bags of them every year for Christmas. Each bite took me back to that kitchen drawer that smelled so good when I opened it. When Mother's stopped making those cookies, I mourned the loss of a childhood friend.

All through the '60s, while Dad and Mom and Opal and Dale played endless hands of pinochle late into the night on Saturdays, I was in the living room by myself, watching black-and-white movies on the late show. That was how my passion for old

Hollywood was kindled. I would lie on the sofa in the dark while the lights from the TV danced on the walls all around me and be transfixed by the cowboys and Indians, the gangsters, the scary monsters. And even through the screams and the loud bangs of gunfire on the television, I could hear the reassuring sounds of my four "parents" in the next room laughing and telling stories. There was no better, more life-affirming sound to listen to as I drifted off to sleep.

~

The story of how we learned Doug's Family Secret has been told so many times that I'm sure some parts have been embellished. It feels like legend now. But this is what I remember hearing.

It began one morning in the spring of 1984. The phone rang at my folks' home in Tehachapi, and Mom answered.

"Is this Frances Griffeth?" a male voice asked.

"Yes." She was thinking *salesman* and was getting ready to hang up.

"Are you related to Dale Griffeth?"

Mom hesitated. She and Dad hadn't seen Dale and Opal in years. The two couples had drifted apart. Mom and Dad were living on their farm 100 miles north of Los Angeles, and Dale and Opal were living in a coastal community in central California.

"Yes, I know Dale," Mom said. "He's my brother-in-law. Why? Who is this?"

"Do you remember a child born to Dale and Opal Griffeth in December of 1942?"

What in the world . . .

"Yes, I do," she said. "He died."

"Actually, he didn't die," said the voice. "I am that child."

Mom thought back to that time. In the spring of 1942, just as the United States was becoming involved in World War II, Dale and Opal left Kansas with their four small children and joined my parents in Los Angeles. By then, Dad was working on the Yellow Line streetcars, and he helped Uncle Dale land a job as a bus driver. Not long after they arrived in California, Opal discovered that she was pregnant.

She went into labor sometime between Christmas and New Year's. Dale dropped their children off with Mom and Dad and took Opal to the hospital, where she gave birth to a boy. Dale called my parents from the hospital with terrible news. The infant had been stillborn, he said. Everyone was devastated.

Mom later recalled that for years after, Opal at odd moments would say strange things like, "I wonder whatever happened to that baby?"

"He's in heaven, Opal," Mom always assured her. But she wondered why Opal kept asking.

It turned out the baby wasn't in heaven. He was in Southern California. The boy born to Opal and Dale had not died. When Opal learned she was pregnant, she insisted that they could not afford another child, and apparently Uncle Dale agreed. So they quietly made arrangements for an adoption. A doctor and his wife took the infant and raised him with their other children. When he turned 40, the now grown-up boy felt it was time to find his biological family. His adoptive mother gave him the names of his birth parents and he began his search.

After a few dead ends, he located Dale and Opal. He telephoned out of the blue one afternoon and Dale answered.

"I thought this day might come," Dale said to him over the phone. But he would not allow his long-lost son to speak to his mother. Opal had just turned 70 and she had recently had a minor heart episode. Dale thought the news would be too distressing for her.

The ever-persistent son then reached out to my parents. My mother was skeptical about this man being who he said he was, so a meeting was arranged on neutral ground, at the home of Mom and Dad's minister. Dad later told me that the moment he saw this stranger, he knew he was a Griffeth, and he enthusiastically welcomed him to the family with a big bear hug.

My eldest sister, Barbara, took our cousin Donna to lunch and revealed the astonishing news about the brother Donna didn't know she had. Donna had been 10 years old when that baby was born, and she vividly remembered living through the tragic aftermath. But now here he was, alive, and she was speechless. She went home and told the rest of her siblings, who greeted the news with amazement and excitement.

When it was my turn to be introduced to this new cousin, we gathered at my parents' house. I had the same reaction Dad did. When I walked into the living room where everyone was waiting, I came face to face with a man who looked just like my uncle and my father. There was indeed no question that he was a Griffeth.

I extended my hand to him.

"I'm Bill," I said. "Welcome, cousin."

He laughed and shook my hand.

"Thank you," he said. "Call me Doug."

I wasn't there the day Doug met his biological family for the first time. They all gathered at Donna's home, and by all accounts, everyone was happy to meet him except Aunt Opal. Doug told me later that he overheard her refer to him as "the stranger." I understood. And so did he. He was, after all, the living reminder of a painful episode in her life that she had wanted to leave behind. The family now knew about the unthinkable decision she had made to give up her own child, and she would be exposed to judgment. And she no doubt imposed the harshest judgment of all on herself. The older, more mature Opal had to have been ashamed about what the younger Opal had done. This was her "mistake."

Initially, Opal simply wanted Doug and the whole episode to disappear. But he didn't go away. His siblings welcomed him enthusiastically, and eventually she also warmed to him. But she was still my outspoken Aunt Opal. Doug told the story of how, during a family card game, when he beat his mother in an especially competitive hand, she pointed a finger at him, squinted her eyes, and said, "You know, if abortion had been legal back in the day, you wouldn't be here." He still laughs when he tells that story.

Doug caught the genealogy bug around the same time I did, in the summer of 2003. He turned out to be a tenacious researcher, and his greatest asset was that he was such a people person. While I was happy to spend hours by myself quietly digging through records, Doug loved to reach out to living relatives, collecting old family photos and anecdotes in the process. And because he had an aptitude for science, which I did not share, he developed an interest in DNA testing and used it to find previously unknown relations.

Doug was especially excited to be a part of our ancestor hunt through Kansas in August 2012. He enjoyed hiking through cemeteries and taking pictures of ancestral landmarks, and more than once he struck up conversations with locals in diners and motels explaining what we were doing in Kansas while Cindy and Chuck and Terryll and I shyly stayed to ourselves. But most important for him, he went to Kansas to get a better sense of who Dale and Opal were. We passed by the many homes they had rented during the early years of their marriage. It turned out that each of his four older birth siblings was born in a different house. Why had they moved so many times, Doug wondered aloud one afternoon. Had they struggled that much financially?

"Maybe there is something to the notion that they just couldn't afford to have another mouth to feed," he said to me as we passed by yet another house his birth parents had lived in.

I have always been fascinated by Doug. He had been exiled by his own mother and father yet somehow he was not bitter about it. His adoptive parents had, after all, given him a good life. He had attended a prestigious university (something none of his Griffeth siblings did), and he enjoyed his career in the entertainment business. He carried with him a worldly wisdom that allowed him to accept his birth mother's fateful decision long before she could accept it herself.

I was drawn to Doug for another reason. He was the fifth child in his birth family, just as I was. There was an odd symmetry to Mom and Dad's and Dale and Opal's broods. Both couples had their first four children at roughly the same time and in the same order, three daughters and then a son. Four matching pairs. Years later, when I came along, I wanted my own matching cousin but there wasn't one. And then, incredibly, it turned out there was. That had to be one of the reasons Doug and I became fast friends.

And now there was another reason. The complicated and surprising circumstances involving both of our births presented a supreme irony that was not lost on either of us: Doug should in fact be called "Griffeth" but he had a different surname, and now we knew that I was not actually a Griffeth although I *did* have that name. Our strangely unique circumstances deepened the bond between us, and that was why, even though I was upset about it, I could understand Doug's eagerness to contact members of the Wyman family on my behalf. He had already experienced the awkward journey of reaching out to strangers who were his family, and he wanted to help me through it. He meant well, and I appreciated what he had tried to do, but I wasn't ready.

My DNA issue not only gave me a new appreciation of what Doug had gone through but also gave me a new perspective on his mother and my relationship with her. When Mom discovered she was pregnant with me in late 1955, Opal said to her, "Oh Frances, you don't want another child. That would be too much." My dear Aunt Opal, my second mother, the woman who doted on me so much, had cautioned my mother against keeping me. But I get it: I now know it was the Opal of 1942 speaking, as my impending arrival forced her to revisit her own awful dilemma. I have come to believe that while Opal obviously loved me very much, part of the love she felt was love that would have gone to Doug. I was a surprise, just as he had been. Opal had decided she could not—and would not—deal with her surprise. But to Opal's consternation, when Mom was confronted with her surprising, unexpected pregnancy, she made a different choice. I now believe that whenever I was with my aunt, I must have reminded her of the fateful, agonizing decision that she may have come to regret.

In the winter of 1992, not long after Cindy and I moved from Los Angeles to the East Coast, the phone rang late one evening. It was Cousin Donna calling. She apologized for the late hour, but Aunt Opal, whose mind by then had been ravaged by dementia, had announced out of the blue that she wanted to talk to "my Billy." Donna said she had repeatedly tried to comfort her and change the subject, but Opal refused to settle down until she spoke with her Billy.

"Would you mind?" Donna asked.

"Of course not," I said.

She put Opal on the phone.

"Hi, Auntie," I said.

"That's Billy," I heard Donna say in the background. She spoke as if to a child.

"Billy . . ." Aunt Opal slurred my name. She sounded confused.

"How are you, Auntie?" I asked, trying to sound upbeat even as my heart was breaking.

"Billy . . ."

"Yes," said Donna, "that's Billy."

Opal was reaching back to a memory from long ago of a little boy she loved very much. But which little boy?

"I love you, Auntie," I said.

"Billy . . ."

It was the last time I heard her voice. Aunt Opal passed away not long after, at the age of 81. She brought great joy to my childhood, and I know I brought joy to her life as well. I still miss her very much.

CHAPTER 24

Back to "Normal"

February 10, 2013

On Sunday, February 10, I was hunkered down in our family room in New Jersey watching golf on television. It was the final round of the AT&T Pebble Beach National Pro-Am tournament at the Pebble Beach Golf Links in Northern California, maybe the most beautiful golf course in the world. I was feeling sorry for myself, first, because I was stuck indoors with a foot of snow on the ground outside, watching other people enjoying themselves in golf's Garden of Eden. And second, because I was still smarting from our trip to California ten days earlier when I had confronted my mother with my DNA results.

The phone rang. It was Mom calling.

"Are you watching the basketball game?" She sounded cheery, which only deepened my funk. It was as if our uncomfortable conversation in her apartment had never happened. Once again, my mother had successfully compartmentalized her feelings. My DNA issue had been relegated to the secret place in her heart where it may have been hidden my whole life.

I switched the channel to the game she was talking about. The LA Clippers were playing the New York Knicks at Madison Square Garden.

Basketball had been the thing I had shared with my father when I was growing up. But when Dad passed away, Mom suddenly became a sports fan. She started watching all of the teams, both college and professional, that Dad rooted for when he was alive. After Cindy and I left Los Angeles, my interest in LA teams waned. I became a fan of the Yankees, the football Giants, and the Knicks.

"It's a pretty good game," she said of the Clippers-Knicks match. "You should watch."

It was early in the third quarter and the score was tied 58–58. Her team versus my team.

Mom and I chatted while we watched. She asked how much snow we had gotten. I asked how my sister Priscilla was doing. It was all very light and casual. Just like always.

Only it wasn't just like always.

How are you getting along? I wanted her to ask. *Do you have any more questions for me?*

I'm hurting, I wanted to say. *And I have a million questions.*

But she didn't ask. And I didn't bring it up.

"How are Chad and Carlee getting along?" she asked. I told her.

How about me, Mom? Remember our conversation two short weeks ago? Remember your startling revelation about the "mistake" you made when you were younger? Don't you want to know how I'm feeling about that right now?

"Well, I guess I'd better let you go," she said. That was always her signal that she was done talking.

We hung up.

I continued to watch the basketball game, mindful that Mom was watching 2,500 miles away. We were watching it together, just like Dad and I used to do. The Clippers pulled to a four-point lead as the third quarter ended. I had seen enough. I turned back to golf.

Two weeks later, on a Tuesday morning, I was sitting at our kitchen table having breakfast and going through our local newspaper. A story I was reading on the front page jumped to another section. I reached for that section and caught sight of the date printed in the upper right corner of the page: February 26. It hit me: it would have been Dad's ninety-ninth birthday that day. His first birthday since I had learned the truth. In past years on this date I had always picked up the phone and called Mom, and we had reminisced about Dad. But this time I didn't call. And neither did she.

I thought about how much I missed him, even after all the years that he had been gone. This year there was a new dimension to my thoughts; I had new feelings, and a vague sense of unease. I still had wonderful memories of my dad that I cherished, and I still missed him terribly. But now it was more complicated. Not as simple as a son missing his late father on the anniversary of his father's birth. It would never be that simple again. Now I missed more than my father. I also missed the time when I believed he was my father.

Part III

Out of darkness is born the light.

—Saint Catherine of Siena

CHAPTER 25

"Meeting" My Father

March 8, 2013

When I got home from work one evening in early March I found Cindy waiting for me with a file folder. She had pretty much completed her research on the Wyman family, she said. Did I want to know what she had found out?

Up to that point, I had been avoiding the subject altogether, still trying to recover from the trauma of the revelation itself. And deep down, I guess I believed that showing interest in the Wymans was somehow like cheating on my Griffeth heritage. But all the while, Cindy had diligently kept up her research, knowing that the time would come when I would be ready to learn the answers to key questions. Was I ready now?

I said I was. I poured myself a bourbon over ice, we sat down on the sofa in the family room, and I listened while she talked.

Cindy told me my biological father, whose full name I'll say was Eugene Clarence Wyman, was born and raised in Kansas. How ironic. Los Angeles was full of people who had migrated from all over the country, and Mom had happened to connect with one who was from home. I heard God laughing.

But this was actually welcome news. People from Kansas were good people, I told myself, humble people, salt-of-the-earth people. I had demonized this man, convinced that he had forced himself on my mother and made unwanted advances that, for whatever reason, she had not spurned. But a man from Kansas wouldn't do that, I told myself, and I was greatly relieved by this revelation. I wanted—*needed*—Gene Wyman to be an honorable man (or as honorable as the situation permitted).

Cindy continued. He came from a large family and was the fourth of eight children. He had two brothers and five sisters. And he was a good athlete, a standout on his high school baseball team. This was helping. He was coming into focus and he was not a demon. He was a human being with parents and siblings.

In the late 1930s Gene moved from Kansas to California, just like my parents did. My family settled south of downtown LA, and he landed further west, in Santa Monica. Cindy said he worked in the movie industry for a few years. I later searched for him on the Internet Movie Database, and while I found a handful of people named Wyman who had worked behind the scenes, he was not one of them.

What did he do in Hollywood? Did he have visions of becoming a movie star? Is that what drew him to Southern California? Is that kind of drive hereditary? Did my aspirations to work in front of the camera come from this man, this stranger in my genes?

Cindy continued.

Gene Wyman had a complicated personal life, she said. In the fall of 1938 he married wife number one, a woman three years his senior. She was a divorcée with two small children from a previous marriage, and on the day they were married she was already seven months pregnant with Gene's child. Two months later she gave birth to a son they named Gene Jr. Six years after that they had another son they named Richard. So I had two half brothers.

Cindy showed me a 1940 U.S. federal census record. It listed 28-year-old Gene, his 31-year-old wife, her 10-year-old son and 8-year-old daughter, and Gene Jr., age 1½. It said Gene worked in construction, so his time in Hollywood apparently didn't last long. And neither did the marriage. Gene and his first wife divorced after ten years, in June 1948. Three weeks later—*three weeks*—he went to Las Vegas and married wife number two. Less than a year after that, she gave birth to a daughter they named Sandra. So I also had a new half sister.

In the late 1940s, at the same time that my parents bought their farm in the San Fernando Valley, Gene and one of his brothers formed a construction company there. Their venture was prudent, since development in the area started to pick up after World War II.

By 1950 Gene Wyman was a prominent citizen in the Valley. Cindy found an online source of archived newspaper articles from the time that showed he was active in civic and church organizations; for a time he also chaired the local builders' association. In other words, he did all of the things a businessman needed to do to be successful.

In 1958, two years after I was born, the Wyman brothers split up and dissolved their company. Gene and his wife and daughter moved to Arizona, where he started a home-building company. Another prudent move. He had good business instincts.

Cindy found articles and photographs in a local Arizona newspaper that showed Gene and his wife were active in various prominent social circles throughout the 1960s and '70s. Gene was elected president of a local country club, and he won a number of golf trophies. He retired in the 1980s, presumably to a life of leisure.

Suddenly a thought occurred to me: Gene Wyman was the typical CNBC viewer. He was a retired successful businessman who played a lot of golf. Was it possible he watched me on TV? And if he did, did my name ever ring a bell: "Griffeth," an unusual spelling with an e instead of an i? Had he thought of the woman, Fran Griffeth, who worked for him in LA in the '50s, and remembered that she spelled her name the same unusual way?

Fran, could you bring me some paperwork I need?

Did he ever connect the dots? If he did, what was his response? Pride, or panic?

In the best-case scenario, I fantasized, he would respond enthusiastically and welcome me into his life. We would play golf together, and I would become a part of the Wyman family.

In the worst-case scenario, he would be stunned to learn that he had carelessly spawned a bastard son with a woman he had forgotten all about.

But this was all moot because Cindy had one last thing to tell me about Gene Wyman: he had passed away in the late 1990s.

So he was gone. I couldn't reach out to him even if I wanted to.

Now what? What should I do with this information my wife had so painstakingly compiled?

I had two choices. The first choice was to do nothing. I could file the Wyman family information away and continue to live my life as if I were a biological Griffeth. Cindy and I could continue to quietly research the Wyman family and learn more about my true paternal ancestry, but nothing about my life would have to change.

The second choice was to reach out to the Wymans. If I did that, though, what would be my goal? I imagined this was a question adoptees must ask themselves. But in most cases adoptees know for a long time that they were adopted. And for some of them, something was truly missing in their lives and they had vital questions about their biological parents and the life they might have had. Essentially, they were asking, "Who am I? Where did I come from?"

My situation was different. I never felt like anything was missing in my life. What could be achieved by my reaching out to the Wymans? Yes, we would be acknowledging a truth that none of us had known about before. But option two also entailed an obvious emotional risk: what if I reached out to them and they rejected me? I wouldn't blame them. I would be showing up with the troubling news that their father had had an encounter with my mother. It would be very easy to reject the messenger. And if they did that, would I have the resolve to pursue a relationship anyway, the way Doug had, or would I just walk away?

Cindy closed the file folder and set it on the coffee table in front of me. She had done her part. She had found answers to most of the key questions. The next move was mine to make.

I took a sip of my bourbon and swallowed, feeling the burn all the way down.

CHAPTER 26

My New Truth

March 17, 2013

On Saint Patrick's Day, Cindy and I attended a neighborhood party around the corner from our home. The house was full of people we had been acquainted with for years. Our children had all grown up together in the town's schools.

We spent the evening mingling and chatting and generally catching up with everyone. At one point, I was standing in the kitchen looking at family photos posted on the refrigerator. Our hostess walked up. I'll call her Sue. She pointed to a photo of her mother, who had recently passed away at the age of 82. Her mother had been a big fan of mine, she said. I offered my condolences and Sue said she was glad her mother had lived a good long life. I nodded and mentioned that my mother was 95.

"Wow," Sue said. "God bless her. That means you've got good genes. What about your father?"

Yes, what about my father. For years, I had jokingly told people that I hoped I got most of my genes from my mother, because my father started to fall apart at the age of 50. Should I repeat the old refrain to Sue, or should I tell her my new truth?

The pastor of our church had recently preached about living a life of simplicity rather than one of duplicity. In a duplicitous life, he said, you show one face to the public and you wear another in private. At some point you have to decide which one is the real you.

Here was my moment.

"Actually," I said, "my father was in his late eighties when he passed away."

She laughed and said, "Good for you!"

I suspect that if I had been hooked up to an electrocardiograph at that moment, the needle would have been scribbling off the page. My heart was pounding and my breathing was shallow. I felt exposed and vulnerable. I had revealed a deep secret to a neighbor I was only casually acquainted with, and she didn't even know it. And yet, I was telling the truth. It was like I was trying this truth on for the first time. How did it make me feel? I would say I felt unsettled relief. I was glad to be speaking the truth, but it was a truth I was not yet comfortable with.

Sue and I moved on to other topics and the moment passed unnoticed. It had been a good first step. But what about the next time? What was I going to do when someone said, "Tell me about your father"? It was a simple question, but I no longer had a simple answer.

I did a search online—I typed *I found out my father wasn't my father*—to see if others had had this same experience. They had. Up popped a handful of websites on which people related stories similar to mine. I was not alone.

There was the 16-year-old girl who learned her father wasn't her father as her parents were going through an ugly divorce. The truth was revealed to her in a moment of anger—"You're not even my daughter!"—and she was understandably devastated. And there was the 49-year-old man who learned the truth while innocently going through his widowed mother's private letters after she died. Poor guy: there was no one left for him to turn to for answers. And I also came across a long, convoluted essay by a woman who had discovered that her father had somehow maintained two families simultaneously while she was growing up, and in the process she learned that she had a half brother. After several twists and turns she finally found this brother, and he was elated to meet the half sister he hadn't known he had. Eventually they both took DNA tests to learn more about their father's family history and to their dismay they learned that the brother had a different, unknown father. Tragically, the brother died of cancer before he could learn who his actual biological father was.

I was touched by how much these people were willing to reveal to strangers, albeit anonymously, on the websites. This was their way of unburdening themselves of their secret, of releasing the shame they felt about something they hadn't even done. It was something that had been done to *them.* Yet they clearly felt anguished, as if they were the guilty parties. This was their opportunity to publicly reveal their private faces.

One woman who had discovered her father was not her father wrote about her experience at a business conference. On the morning of the first day, as an icebreaker, the facilitator asked everyone to tell the group something unique about themselves that they all might find surprising. She broke out into a sweat. Was now the time, she wondered? Were these the people? When it was her turn, she said, she stood up, took a deep breath, and revealed her secret to the strangers in the room—and she experienced immediate relief.

I now knew how she felt. Telling the truth, even when it's embarrassing, always feels better than keeping it secret.

CHAPTER 27

Mom Makes the First Move

April 5, 2013

I often think about my mother when I cook. I love to cook. She hated it. For me it is a creative outlet; for her it was a chore. When I was growing up she managed an elementary school cafeteria. Her job involved planning, preparing, and serving lunch to hundreds of children, five days a week. She and the woman who worked for her spent each morning rushing around the school's industrial kitchen, chopping and stirring ahead of the lunch bell. Then lunchtime was an hour of chaos: serving the students as they paraded through, and gathering and washing all of the trays by hand after they had finished eating. By the time she got home each evening, I'm sure the last thing Mom wanted to do was cook some more. But she did it anyway. There was always a hot meal for Dad and me at the end of the day, and he and I never set foot in the kitchen. She did it all herself, the prep and the cleanup. And I never heard her complain.

For me, cooking brings great pleasure. Even after a long day at work, I look forward to driving to our local market and planning the evening's dinner menu as I make my way up and down the aisles, sizing up the cuts of meat and the freshness of the produce.

On April 5, a Friday, Cindy and I were preparing dinner in our kitchen at the end of a busy week. Glasses of red wine sat on the counter in front of us, and a half-full bottle stood ready with more. I had changed out of my TV-anchor suit and into sweats, and I was wearing the blue denim apron I wear when I cook. Cindy was tossing some lettuce and tomatoes in a salad bowl, and I was chopping onions and mincing garlic for a marinara sauce. And I thought about my mother.

What gave her pleasure, I wondered? The stories she told about her life usually involved hardships. She was a child of the Depression. Life on the farm involved hard work and lean times, and less than a year after she graduated from high school she was a wife and a mother, which brought new responsibilities.

I sautéed the garlic and onions in some olive oil. Then I added diced plum tomatoes, sliced black olives, and roasted red peppers, and left it all to simmer and thicken. I sipped my wine while I watched the steam rise from the pan, and I breathed in the familiar and reassuring aroma. And in my enjoyment of the moment, I let the world go by.

I doubt very much that Mom ever experienced this kind of simple pleasure. Her life had been almost all work and very little play, which was typical for women of her generation. She was raised on the Protestant work ethic. No joie de vivre. No pleasure without regret.

I put some water on to boil for the pasta, and Cindy and I talked about a trip I would be taking the following week to Los Angeles for a speaking engagement. I would also make time to visit my mother, a visit I was not looking forward to.

"I can't face another trip out there if all we're going to do is act like nothing has changed," I said. "This has gone on too long. I can't bring myself to talk about it on the phone with her, and I know she's never going to bring it up."

Cindy took a sip of her wine while I spoke and then set her glass down on the counter.

"Well, someone has to start the conversation," she said, "and it is probably going to have to be you. What do you want to know?"

"Well, for example, I want to know if she's been thinking about this all these years. When she looked at me as a kid, did she think of him? Do I remind her of him?"

Cindy's eyes began to well up.

"Trust me," she said. "She has thought about it. She's a mother. I'm sure this has been a burden for her for a long time, and I think she buried this deep inside of her. And now it has been discovered, and she is deeply ashamed."

She took another sip of her wine and collected herself. I kept my focus on the sauce.

"You're going to have to be gentle and patient with her," Cindy said. "This will be like digging up a fossil. You can't just use a shovel and start digging. You have to use small tools and brushes and gently remove the dirt."

"I know," I said.

"I hate to see this drive a wedge between you two, and that's what's happening." She was close to sobbing. I could hear it in her voice. "She's your *mother.*"

I stopped what I was doing, looked up, and saw the tears in Cindy's eyes. I knew I could not let this go on forever. This was not how I wanted my relationship with my mother to be during the final years of her life. We were both being stubborn. I was waiting for her to bring up the DNA issue, but it was clear that she didn't want to talk about it. All of the unspoken words lay between us like a pile of broken dishes waiting to be swept away.

The phone rang. Even before the caller ID told us who was on the line, we both knew who it was.

Cindy answered and chatted with my mother for a few minutes. They talked about the kids and the weather and the bad service in her assisted living facility's cafeteria.

"Yes, he's right here," Cindy said as she handed me the phone with an exaggerated smile on her face.

"Your ears must have been burning," I said. "I'm looking forward to seeing you next week."

"I am, too," Mom said. "The weather should be very good. Somewhere between 80 and 85 degrees."

We talked a little more about the weather, and I figured we would move on to other mundane topics. But we didn't.

"I want to say something," she said.

Her tone was deliberate and to the point. I snapped my fingers at Cindy to get her attention. She looked at me, and I gave her a look of anticipation.

"Yes?" I said.

"You are my son," Mom said, "and I love you very much. If you want to tell me things you've discovered about the Wyman family, whether it's good or bad, I want to hear it."

I heaved a huge sigh of relief.

"I'm very glad to hear that, Mom," I said. "I don't know that I have anything bad to tell you about them. I've just wanted to talk about it."

"Of course," she said.

"I've felt like there has been this elephant in the room that we weren't talking about, and it was putting a wall between us, and I don't want that."

"I agree," she said. "I don't want that either."

"How about we talk about it face to face when I get there next week?"

"That sounds great," she said. And she sounded like she meant it.

We hung up and I turned to Cindy. Now there were tears in my eyes.

CHAPTER 28

"Do You Recognize Him?"

April 12, 2013

The next Friday, I landed at Burbank Airport around 2:30 in the afternoon, picked up my rental car, and headed north. Same drill as always. The last time I had taken this trip, in January to celebrate Mom's birthday, I had been a basket case. This time I enjoyed the drive through the desert. It was springtime and orange poppies were blooming everywhere.

Mom and I had made progress. I didn't know where it was all going; I was just glad she was willing to talk. I was certainly anxious to hear what she had to tell me.

I knocked on her apartment door just after 4:30.

"Come in!" she called out. I could hear excitement in her voice.

I opened the door and saw her struggling to rise from her easy chair and take hold of her walker. She was dressed in a purple and white floral print blouse and purple pants. Her name badge was pinned to her blouse to help new neighbors learn her name. She looked bright and happy. We hugged, and her grasp was strong, and she held me for an extra beat. Very unlike the last time.

We chatted enthusiastically, making small talk about my flight and her pretty outfit and what a beautiful day it was and how her cat was doing and on and on. Chuck and Terryll were coming over in an hour to take us out to dinner, so Mom and I had time to talk before they arrived. I sat down on the sofa next to her chair, she turned off the TV, and we got down to business.

"I'm so glad you called the other day," I said.

"I just feel so bad for you in all of this," she said.

I felt a catch in my throat. Finally.

"Well, this has to be so hard for you, too," I said. "I'm sorry we are having to go through this, but I'm glad we can talk about it now."

"Yes, we can," she said. Her voice was strong. "Whatever you want to talk about." The months of ice were melting away.

I looked her dead in the eye.

"First of all, I want you to know that nothing has changed. Everything will be the same."

I'm not sure I believed those words. I had no idea if things would change between my mother and me. We were both still swimming in turbulent waters, tossed about by this storm of confusion and deception, trying urgently to keep our heads above the surface as we searched for solid footing. There were no guarantees about how long it would take, or where we would find ourselves once the storm had passed. In the meantime, I wanted her to feel protected from harm.

She looked relieved to hear my assurances.

"I agree," she said. "Nothing has changed."

And so we began. I told her what Cindy had uncovered about Gene Wyman, about how he was born in Kansas.

"Isn't that funny?" I said. "Of all places."

She nodded and looked mildly surprised.

I told her about his first marriage to the older woman with the two children, the birth of his two sons, the divorce, his quick remarriage to his second wife, and the birth of a daughter.

She nodded some more, but still she said nothing. I couldn't tell if this was making her uncomfortable.

"And then he and his wife and daughter moved to Arizona in 1958," I said.

"Arizona," she repeated. "Did his brother go with him?" she asked.

The answer was no.

"Did Gene ever talk about his family?" I asked.

"No. His brother told me he had two sons by his first wife."

"Did he ever talk about his daughter?" I asked.

"No. All that I knew came from his brother."

She talked about the business. It sounded like Wyman Construction was pretty much a small two-man operation. Mom had worked in the front office as the bookkeeper and office manager, and the brothers each had their own offices.

"They fought once in a while," she said. "They would close the door and I would hear them arguing. I never knew what it was about."

I picked up my iPad and asked her if she wanted to see the photo we had found of Gene.

She nodded. "Okay," she said tentatively. She had agreed to this conversation, but clearly it was awkward for her. We were tiptoeing through forbidden territory.

I brought up the only image I had of my biological father. It was the shot of the group of businessmen taken in the early 1950s that Cindy and I had come across online. There were ten men in the photo, all dressed in business suits, all looking earnest and professional. All except one: Gene Wyman. The photographer had caught him looking away from the camera, in profile, and unlike the other men, he was laughing. All of which made him stand out. But my eyes were drawn to him for a different reason. He looked like me. This stranger actually looked like me. That was my profile, and that was my smile.

I placed the photo in front of Mom and watched her face carefully. I was anxious to see what her reaction would be when she laid eyes on him for the first time in almost sixty years.

She studied the photo. Her expression didn't change, and she didn't say a word. She just stared. The photo was taken around the time she and Gene had known each other. I wondered if it was jogging memories she hadn't thought of in a long time.

"Do you recognize him?" I prompted.

She pointed to the man seated next to Gene.

I was stunned.

"That's not him," I said, trying not to betray my surprise. I pointed to Gene.

She didn't say anything at first. Then: "That doesn't look like him. His hair wasn't that dark."

I explained that maybe the black and white photo made it look darker.

"Was he blond?" I asked, wondering if he and I shared the same hair color.

"No," she said. "It was about the same as mine," meaning a light shade of brown.

I waited to see if she said anything else, hoping she would launch into a story. But she didn't. I asked if she recognized any of the other men in the photo, hoping to dislodge a memory. Any memory. But she didn't know any of them. I read their names out loud from the photo's caption. Nothing clicked.

That was it. The photograph was a dead end. No memories. No stories.

I set the iPad aside and tried to get her to open up in other ways, but no luck. The well was dry. Despite her assurance that she would talk about whatever I wanted, I suspected that her embarrassment about all of it kept her from sharing more. Maybe just talking about Gene Wyman felt like cheating on Dad all over again. And despite my insistence that nothing would change between us, maybe she felt the risk of alienating me if I knew more of the particulars of what she had done.

Or maybe she just didn't remember. Whatever the case, although the air had cleared between us, not much was revealed.

There was a knock at the door. My brother and his wife had arrived; it was time for supper. Our conversation was over for the moment.

CHAPTER 29

My New Family History

April 20, 2013

“Are you sure?” Cindy asked as she handed me the memory stick.

“I’m sure,” I assured her. I inserted it into my computer and opened the folder labeled “Wyman Family.”

I had decided it was time that I came to terms with my past, so I asked Cindy to give me all the information she had accumulated. I wanted to spend time carefully studying the records and beginning the process of immersing myself in this phantom heritage of mine.

There were three files inside the folder on my computer screen. One contained photographs. Another included census records that extended back to the early 1800s. And there was an Excel file labeled “Wyman Family History.” My wife the accountant had done a thorough job of organizing the data.

I started with the Excel file, expecting the chart would be in chronological order, beginning somewhere in the 1800s and moving forward. But it wasn’t. Instead, it was in reverse chronological order. The first entry was for Gene Wyman’s immediate family.

“Gene Wyman” was the main heading.

The first subhead was “Wife #1.” There was her name along with the dates of their marriage and divorce. Below that were their two sons, Gene Jr. and Richard, their birth years, and information about their spouses and children.

The second subhead was “Wife #2.” Below that was their daughter, Sandra, and the year of her birth.

There was also a place for a third subhead, but there was no heading. Cindy had simply listed my mother’s name and, below it, my name with my date of birth, followed by the year that Cindy and I got married, and then below that Chad and Carlee and their birthdates.

I felt a dull ache in my gut where the original DNA punch had landed months earlier. Cindy was getting way ahead of herself, I thought. We didn't belong on this chart. But I was wrong. Whether or not Mom wanted to acknowledge it, and whether or not I wanted to accept it, this was the truth. I was the son of Gene Wyman and Frances Griffeth. Seeing it in print this way was so unsettling. It was as if my mother and I were outcasts in a Dickens novel, a ne'er-do-well woman and her young son, looking in on the Wyman family as they went about their lives oblivious to our existence.

I scrolled down to the earlier generations. The Wymans had large families. There were Gene's parents—my grandparents—and their eight children. Next came my great-grandparents and their eleven children. And finally my great-great-grandfather, who had thirteen children with his first wife; then, after she died, he remarried and had twelve more children. So many relatives. And all of them just names on a page.

Before they arrived in Kansas in the 1870s, my line of the Wyman family lived for several years in Tennessee. I didn't know what it meant to be from Tennessee. I was used to my people being from New England and New York. They were Puritans and Pilgrims and Quakers. I had visited their towns and walked their streets. I had driven their back roads. Their homeland was my homeland.

I had been to Tennessee only once, when I gave a speech in Chattanooga years ago, in the mid-1990s. I flew into Atlanta that day, drove north just over the Georgia-Tennessee border to Chattanooga, gave my lunchtime speech, and then immediately turned around and headed south again, back to Atlanta. That was it. Now Cindy's research showed that I had deep roots there. My biological fourth great-grandfather, Jonathan Wyman, lived in northern Tennessee with his wife Rosemary and their children in the late 1700s, and different lines of Wymans have lived there ever since.

How did I feel about all of these strangers I shared a bloodline with? I felt nothing. No connection at all. Initially I told myself it was because I hadn't done this research myself. I hadn't made these discoveries and accumulated these records, Cindy had. But that wasn't the real reason. The real reason I didn't feel anything for these people was because I didn't want to be a Wyman. I wanted to be a Griffeth.

I opened Cindy's file of photographs. I had expected to see fuzzy old sepia-toned pictures of relatives from the distant past. Instead, she had accumulated a collection of modern photos of Gene Wyman's grandchildren—my nieces and nephews—that she had found on Facebook. And there were also pictures of their children, Gene Wyman's great-grandchildren.

One person in particular caught my eye. I will call her Rachel. She was the eldest of the great-grandkids, born in 1991, making her the same age as Carlee. Instinctively I did a quick calculation: Rachel and Carlee were first cousins once removed. Cindy had included a link to Rachel's Facebook page, and I clicked on it. Her profile photo showed a young woman with a bright smile and long, sandy-blonde hair. The "About Rachel" section said she was a senior in college. A photo on her Facebook timeline immediately got my attention. It was a picture of Rachel with her grandfather—"It's my grandpa!" she'd written—Gene Wyman Jr. My brother. Rachel had uploaded the photo only the day before. This was not history. This was now.

I studied the photograph. Gene Jr. and I didn't exactly resemble each other; instead, we suggested each other. Like me, he was not a big man. He looked to be of average height and build. And he didn't look his age, which was 75. He still had the trim body and muscle tone of a man years younger. The shape of his face, the placement of his cheekbones, and the strength of his jaw line were all familiar. He had my high forehead and receding hairline, but his hair was much darker than mine, and it was slicked back in a style he had probably worn since he was a kid in the 1940s. He wore old-fashioned aviator reading glasses, and the glasses case was tucked into the breast pocket of his dress shirt. In other words, his style was practical, not trendy. He wasn't trying to make a fashion statement. He was his own man. Take me or leave me, the photo said.

I shared features with Gene Jr., just as I shared features with Chuck. My two brothers were only two years apart in age, and it struck me that they looked nothing alike. But why would they?

They weren't related. I was the link between them. There was some of me in each of them, features that Gene and I shared with our father and features that Chuck and I shared with our mother.

I noticed that my breathing was becoming shallow. I felt a heaviness in my chest. I took a couple of deep breaths, but the heaviness persisted. I was having a mild anxiety attack. I guess I felt guilty stalking these people like this, I told myself. I was a Peeping Tom invading their personal lives. But there was another reason: this was all becoming very real. Here, right in front of me, were members of my biological family. And it would be so easy to connect with them, I thought. All I had to do was click on the Add Friend button on Rachel's Facebook page. That would start the ball rolling. But I couldn't do it. My curiosity was superseded by my fear of unknown consequences. It was a dilemma I had been wrestling with for several weeks. Some of my friends had cautioned me about reaching out to people I didn't know. How would they react when they discovered they were related to a television personality? Would they try to take advantage of me and possibly complicate my career as well as my life?

I studied the Facebook photo of Gene Jr. and his granddaughter. They seemed like nice people, and they looked so happy. Would they still be smiling when I showed up suddenly with my story? Would they laugh at the absurdity of it all, or would they be resentful?

An idea came to me. I closed the browser on my computer, opened the word processing software to a blank page, and began to type.

CHAPTER 30

Dear Mr. Wyman

April 20, 2013

Dear Mr. Wyman,

I'm going to assume you've never received a letter quite like this. I know I've never written one like it.

To get to the point, I have reason to believe that you and I are half brothers. Here's why:

In the summer of 2012 I took a DNA test at the behest of my first cousin. He and I are amateur genealogists, and he uses DNA for part of his research. When my test came back, we were shocked to find that my results did not match his when they should have been nearly identical. I then had my brother take a DNA test. His results matched our cousin, but he did not match me. I was the odd man out.

I presented the results to my 95-year-old mother and she confessed that she made a "mistake" when she was younger. I am the result of that mistake.

From 1953–55, Mom worked for Wyman Construction. She told me that during the fall of '55 she and your father had a brief affair and when she became pregnant she quit her job. I was born in the summer of 1956. To the best of my knowledge your father never knew that I existed.

I have one request. I'm wondering if you would be willing to talk or correspond with me to tell me about your father. I already have some information about him. My wife has done research online and discovered quite a bit about your family's history going all the way back to Tennessee. I have a photo of him we found online that was taken when he was a member of a builders association in Los Angeles. I would appreciate seeing more.

I'm sure this is all very unsettling to you. I understand. I've spent the past 18 months getting used to it. And you might be skeptical. I understand that, too. If you are willing, I will pay for you to take a DNA test. I suspect your results will be nearly identical to mine.

I wouldn't blame you if you chose not to respond to this letter but I hope you do. I'm willing to keep this between the two of us. You wouldn't have to share this with the rest of your family if you didn't want to. I'm not looking to insinuate myself into your family's life. I already have a family. My only aim is to learn something about the man who was my biological father.

Thank you for your consideration.

Sincerely,
Bill Griffeth

When I finished the letter I printed a copy, signed my name at the bottom, folded the page in thirds and tucked it in an envelope. After I sealed it, I began to carefully address it by hand. I've never had very good handwriting. My teachers in school were always onto me about that. And because we now type everything, it has only gotten worse for lack of practice. Legible handwriting used to mean something. It made a good impression. That's what I wanted to do with Gene Wyman Jr. In the photo of him on his granddaughter's Facebook page, he looked like a reasonable guy. An approachable guy. One who would respond to my revelation in a calm, thoughtful manner.

I took my time and tried to form each letter carefully on the envelope. When I was finished I studied the final product. It didn't flow. It looked tortured and rushed. But I also wondered if it would seem familiar to him and perhaps resemble handwriting he had seen in his past.

I placed a stamp on the envelope and left it sitting on my desk. I wanted to sleep on it before I sent it. If I sent it.

CHAPTER 31

"Are You Taking Notes?"

May 12, 2013

I called my mother one Sunday afternoon just to chat. All of the usual topics came up: the weather, family gossip, and bad dining hall food. She sounded especially cheery, which prompted me to make a spur-of-the-moment decision I later regretted. Since she was in such a good mood, I decided to take another stab at asking her some questions about Gene Wyman, but this time I would not come at them directly. I would try a different strategy. I started by telling her that I wanted to know about all of the jobs she had had over the years. I was always asking questions about things like that as part of my effort to record our family history. And even though I thought I could already recite most of the jobs she had ever held, I figured this would be a painless way to learn more about the one job—and boss—I was really interested in.

We started at the beginning. After she and her parents left the farm and moved to town in 1930, Mom attended Washington High School, and she got an after-school job ironing shirts for the town doctor, Fred LeMaster, and doing light housekeeping for his wife, Marvel.

"I ironed five shirts each week and was paid 50 cents," Mom said.

For Marvel, she washed dishes and mopped the kitchen floor. "Mrs. LeMaster was meticulous. She was always reminding me not to forget to mop the corners of the floor."

"Huh," I said, trying to sound interested.

She didn't get her next job until the 1940s, during WWII, when she and Dad and my siblings lived south of downtown Los Angeles. Mom began to reminisce about that time and that neighborhood, now part of East LA, telling stories I had heard a million times. I was going to have to be patient.

The home my family lived in at that time, she said, was one of a group built in the early twentieth century. When the city decided to build a coliseum in memory of soldiers who had died in World War I, they chose to build it in that neighborhood, and instead of tearing the houses down to make room, they had moved all of them—including the one my family later lived in—onto a vacant parcel of land several blocks south. The Los Angeles Memorial Coliseum, completed in 1923, later hosted two summer Olympics, in 1932 and 1984.

The landlord Mom and Dad rented from owned other relocated homes in the same neighborhood, and he hired Mom to act as a "super," calling repairmen as needed and generally serving as the landlord's eyes and ears. In return my parents got a break on their rent.

Mom continued her familiar story. After the war, when they bought their three-acre farm in the San Fernando Valley, she went to work for the local nursery. Her assignment was to plant seedlings in small pots that were sold to local supermarkets. It was a cold, wet job, she said.

"Where was the nursery located?" I asked.

"The address was 3000 something," she said. "I can't remember the name of the street."

The nursery owners decided to build a roof over the area where they potted the plants, for some protection from the cold temperatures and gusting winds. Very matter-of-factly Mom mentioned that the contractor hired to build the roof was Gene Wyman. I sat up. She was volunteering this without my asking. Maybe we really were making progress.

When his team finished building the roof, Gene told Mom that if she ever got tired of her job at the nursery, she could come work for him. Which is what she did. She joined Wyman Construction as office manager in 1953.

"Did you enjoy your work at the nursery?" I asked. I was dying to move on to her next job, but I remained patient and kept my tone casual.

She did enjoy it, she said. She had always loved plants, and she had a very green thumb. If conditions had been better, she said, she might have stayed longer.

And I wouldn't be here, I thought.

"How about Wyman Construction?" I finally asked, trying to sound nonchalant. "Did you enjoy that job?"

"Not really," she deadpanned. "It was just a job."

Silence.

"Really," I said, waiting for more.

"Yeah," she said. Nothing.

"What is this for?" she asked, now slightly irritated. "Are you taking notes?"

That was it. We had ventured too close to the sensitive area. She had seen through my little charade, so I retreated and moved on to her final job managing the elementary school cafeteria, which she did for almost twenty years, until she retired in 1980.

And then we hung up.

So that was how she and Gene Wyman met. She hadn't applied for the job, it had been offered to her. I'm guessing she accepted because an office job sounded more appealing, and the pay had to have been better. But was there more to it than that?

Why would he offer the job to a woman who had no prior experience? This had "playful flirtation" written all over it. At the time, Mom was in her mid-30s, she had been married for seventeen years, and she had four teenagers at home. She was probably flattered by the interest this man showed in her.

And what was his motivation? I wondered. What, indeed.

Thirty minutes after our conversation ended, the phone rang.

"It's your mother," Cindy called out when she saw the caller ID, and she picked it up.

"Yup, he's right here," she said as she handed me the phone.

"Hi," I said.

"It was 3000 Oakwood Avenue," Mom said. She had remembered the address of the nursery.

"Did you look it up?" I asked.

"No, I sat here and thought about it, and it just came to me."

"Good job! Thanks."

I started to say good-bye, but she wasn't finished.

"Am I ever going to see you again?" she asked plaintively.

My heart sank. I had indeed gone too far with my questions about her job at the construction company. She knew exactly what it was all about. I was still thinking about my biological father, and her greatest fears were surfacing once again. She was afraid that I was angry with her and that I would stop visiting her. This was precisely what I hadn't wanted to happen.

That's when it hit me. I had been so obsessed with my paternity, so focused on two men who had both been gone for a long time, that I was neglecting the one parent I still had. The day my mother confessed her youthful indiscretion to me, I somehow stopped being her son and I became an adversary. An interrogator determined to get to the bottom of my DNA issue.

I made a decision on the spot: it was time to let go. There would be no more questions for her about my birth father. No more awkward moments and no more painful visits to that awful time. I had gone as far as I was going to go on this journey with her. The unspeakable would remain unspoken. I would never again mention her "mistake."

I also knew that I would not be sending that letter I had written to my half brother, Gene Wyman Jr. At least not while Mom was alive. It was time to put the issue aside and leave her in peace. She deserved it.

CHAPTER 32

Finding My Father

June 9, 2013

Cindy and I flew to Phoenix on a Sunday in early June, when temperatures there were already hitting triple digits with regularity. After we landed, we picked up our rental car and headed out of town. I wanted to see where Gene Wyman and his family lived from the late 1950s until his death in the late 1990s. It was time for me to take some action. No more ruminating. No more feeling sorry for myself. And since I had resolved not to ask my mother any more questions, I knew I was going to have to find answers without her. I would start in Arizona.

I was in search of context. Context was important to me. It was part of my self-identity. When I was growing up, California was my whole world, and as I grew older that world was extended to include Kansas and Colorado, where my grandmothers and aunts and uncles lived. When I married Cindy, her native South Dakota also became part of my identity. After we moved to the East Coast and I began my genealogical research, I added Massachusetts and New York, where my earliest Griffeth ancestors lived in the seventeenth and eighteenth centuries, and then the states they migrated through in the nineteenth century: Ohio, Illinois, and Nebraska.

And now I could add Arizona, where my biological father lived for half of his life and where he died and was buried. Exploring this part of the country was something I could do without bothering anybody by asking embarrassing questions.

I love driving through the open desert. The vast expanse is so liberating. On that Sunday there wasn't a cloud in the deep blue sky, and the thermometer on the dashboard said it was 107 degrees outside. Arizona has long been a land of independent thinkers. In the late 1950s it was the home of Senator Barry Goldwater and the modern conservative movement. Was Gene Wyman one of those independent thinkers? Is that why the

Wymans moved here, I wondered as the Joshua trees whizzed by. Did he see a business opportunity here? Was it an escape?

When we arrived in the town where the Wymans lived so long ago, we went straight to our hotel to check in. The hotel was in the heart of the older portion of town, an area that was still developing when the Wyman family moved here. And, as it happened, it was only one block from the cemetery where I knew Gene and his wife were buried.

It was late afternoon. We had time to drive around a bit to get the lay of the land before supper. So we got back in the car just as the sun was heading toward the western horizon, making it the hottest part of the day.

Our first destination was the cemetery. We had no idea where the Wymans' graves were located and it was too hot to get out of the car to hunt, so we just drove through. We planned to come back early one morning when the temperature was more tolerable. The cemetery was large, extending for several acres in all directions. We drove slowly along the main road that bisected the property, past the motley assortment of monuments and flower arrangements and flags.

I felt a presence, as I often do when I'm visiting ancestral graveyards. He was here, and I could feel him. My heart pounded in my chest. This was an important moment, and I knew it. It was the first time I had felt a physical connection to my Wyman heritage.

I slowed the car to a crawl as I surveyed the sea of headstones. What was I doing the day my father died, I wondered. Gene Wyman passed away on a Sunday in the fall. There was a good chance I was playing golf that afternoon. Is that what I was doing when my father breathed his last, playing a game that he and I both loved? Did I feel a shadow pass over my heart that day and wonder what it was about?

And what about the day of his funeral? It was probably held a few days later, maybe that Wednesday or Thursday. Presumably his children and grandchildren were together here at the cemetery to mourn his passing. But for his youngest son, it had been just another day. At that time, I was hosting the midday show on CNBC, *Power Lunch*. Was I on the air, casually talking about the stock market, as his funeral procession made its way from the church to this cemetery and his family gathered around his grave?

We passed through the exit and I turned onto the busy road that bordered the cemetery. We would be back.

The town where the Wymans settled reminded us a lot of the San Fernando Valley. It was an aging bedroom community that was past its prime. It probably went through the same cycle that the Valley did: a sleepy beginning with lots of agriculture, then small growth, then big growth as the open land was gradually replaced by housing, then wild growth, then expansion to accommodate further growth. Meanwhile, the early areas of development had begun to deteriorate because there was no incentive to redevelop. There was only more expansion.

Gene Wyman's company built hundreds of homes and a couple of apartment complexes in this Arizona town, all of them constructed in the 1960s and '70s. Before our trip, Cindy searched the archives of the local newspaper going back to the early 1960s and found ads for model houses built by Wyman Homes. The ads included addresses, which helped us find them during our tour. Most of them were still standing, but they were showing their age. All were classic 1960s suburban desert homes with stucco walls and tile roofs. Modern at the time, and affordable.

Each of Gene's model homes had the same distinct feature: a pair of palm trees planted on either side of the front walk. This, apparently, was his signature. Back in the day, it had represented a touch of elegance for the affordable homes. By now, though, all of the palm trees had grown to heights way out of proportion to the modest-size yards they were planted in. They towered over the houses and now looked out of place and even grotesquely comical.

We also found the house Gene and his family lived in. It was another classic ranch-style house that had once upon a time been a respectable home for a successful businessman and his family. Now, it was nice but not spectacular. We drove past slowly enough to study its features but not so slow as to draw attention. An iron fence surrounded the front yard and, of course, there were two overgrown palm trees standing sentry on either side of the front gate. When we got to the end of the street, I turned the car around and drove past a second time. But I wasn't really looking at the house. The Wymans probably hadn't lived there in thirty years, and a lot had changed. Instead, I was trying to take in the significance of the place and of the moment. This was where my biological father was living when I reached important milestones in my life, when I graduated from high school and college in the 1970s, and when Cindy and I got married in the spring of 1982. For him, though, they were just regular days.

We turned the corner and headed toward the country club Gene belonged to years ago. It was in the older part of town, surrounded by large homes that in the 1950s and 1960s had housed the upper crust of the city. Wyman Homes had built some of these places. They had once been showcases, but now they all looked tired and neglected.

I had a very specific reason for visiting the club, beyond wanting to see where Gene Wyman had spent so much of his time. I had a hunch we would find a photograph of him there. He was the club's president for a time many years ago, and my guess was they would have a wall of photos of past presidents somewhere in the clubhouse, as many private clubs do. I needed to see those photos.

We pulled into the parking lot, which was virtually empty. It was around ten in the morning on a Monday, typically a slow day for private golf clubs. I parked in the shade of a eucalyptus tree, and we got out and walked through the front door of the clubhouse.

"What are we going to say if someone asks us what we're doing here?" Cindy asked.

"We'll think of something," I said.

But no one asked. We acted like we belonged, and it seemed to work.

It was a classic vintage country club, just as I'd thought it would be. There were plush easy chairs and sofas in the sitting area, and framed photos and plaques hanging on the paneled walls. We peeked into the dining room where the wait staff was setting tables, getting ready for lunch. People in golf attire walked past us, and we nodded and smiled.

I saw a sign that said "Pro Shop" with an arrow pointing down a hallway. We headed in that direction. The locker rooms were to the right and the pro shop was on the left. We turned left, and there, just as I had hoped, was the wall of photographs of the club's past presidents. My heart leaped. We carefully inspected each one until we found our man. It was taken when he was twenty years older than he was in the group photo we already had of him, and he looked it. His hair had thinned, and the dark-rimmed glasses he wore, more practical than fashionable, added years to his features. In the earlier photo he was laughing. Then he had the look of a cocky, carefree young man who was full of energy and promise. In this new photo he looked settled and he had the confident appearance of a successful businessman. He was wearing a dark suit and a narrow black tie, styles that are fashionably retro today.

I looked at the date next to his name and did a quick calculation. He was roughly 59 years old when the picture was taken, three years older than I was at that moment. Did we look alike? Yes and no. The shape of our head was the same; those were definitely my eyes; that was my chin and my jaw line, and that was my forehead with the same receding hairline. And I noted that his temples had gone gray in precisely the same pattern mine had. But that was not my nose, and those were most definitely not my ears. They were huge.

"If I had those ears," I whispered to Cindy, "I would have had a terrific career in radio."

I took several close-up pictures of the photo with my Blackberry, making sure I got the correct angle and that everything was in focus. Mission accomplished, I thought, with great satisfaction. I had my picture.

We continued to the pro shop, where a young man in his late twenties was working behind the counter.

"Can I help you?" he asked in a friendly manner. He had close-cropped brown hair and wore a bright yellow golf shirt.

I had already rehearsed my story.

"We are from out of town. An old family friend belonged to the club many years ago, and we wanted to see it."

"What was his name?"

"Gene Wyman," I said, and I immediately panicked. I hadn't completely thought this through. What if this young man said, "Gene Wyman! That's my grandfather!" Or, "What a coincidence.

His son just came through here. He's about to tee off. Let me go get him." What would we do then?

But he didn't say any of that. The name didn't ring a bell, and I exhaled with relief.

"Welcome to our club," he said. "Take a look around."

And so we did. We walked outside, where a handful of golfers were milling about waiting to begin their rounds. All of them were dressed in shorts and light-colored golf shirts, and most of them wore wide-brimmed hats to protect their faces from the desert sun. I scanned the groups, picking out the oldest men, wondering which of them had been around when Gene played here. Would they recognize the name Wyman?

The golf course was in great shape. The fairways were lush and green and well-manicured, and the white bunkers shone in the bright sunlight. It all looked very inviting. Cindy followed me to the first tee. It was slightly elevated, offering a clear view of several holes. I looked down the first fairway toward the green. It was a relatively short, easy par 4. First holes are not typically very challenging. They are meant to be like a friendly handshake at the beginning of a round, and that's what this was.

This was what Gene had seen every time he started a new round. I pictured the first hole at my own club and thought about the excitement I always feel just before I hit that first drive. Gene probably felt the same thing when he stood where I was standing. I took a picture of the view to help me remember the moment. Then Cindy took pictures of me with the golf course and the golfers and the palm trees and the blue sky all behind me. I lingered for a bit, and Cindy gave me my space. I didn't want to leave. This was sacred ground. I wanted to play a round of golf here and walk where my father had walked hundreds of times. He probably had stories about each hole. About long putts made and short putts missed, the bad shots that made him want to quit the game and the good ones that brought him back. I felt a lump in my throat. This was probably as close as I would ever get to Eugene Wyman. And it really wasn't all that close.

I heard the sound of golf carts behind me. A new foursome was pulling up to begin their round. I turned back to Cindy, but I couldn't look her in the eye. Together we walked off the tee box.

"Any chance I could buy a few things?" I asked the young man behind the counter when we reentered the pro shop.

"Absolutely," he said. "In fact, I'll give you the members' discount in honor of your friend."

I picked out a couple of shirts with the club logo on the sleeve and a handful of logoed ball markers. They would be my secret little souvenirs when I played back home, reminding me of Gene each time I got ready to putt.

The young man put everything in a bag, thanked us for coming, and we were on our way.

Later in the day we drove to the east side of town. Cindy had dug up the home address of Gene's younger son, Richard, who still lived in the area. His home was in a newer development. So far as we could tell from online records, he and his wife lived alone. They were both in their late sixties, so if they had children they were probably grown and out of the house.

It was after sunset when we turned onto their street. Automatic lights were starting to come on as the sky gradually changed from blue to orange to black. We counted down to Richard's address using the street numbers on the curb. It was near the end of a quiet cul-de-sac: a nice street. The lawns were all well manicured. The cars in the driveways were mostly new models.

We passed by Richard's house then circled back and slowed to a stop in front of it. Another classic desert design: pink stucco, flat roof, and rounded arched entry to the front porch. We were amused to see that there were not two but three palm trees planted in the front yard.

I snapped a couple of photos, intending to study them later. I hadn't planned to linger. I did not want to draw attention and raise suspicion. But something made me stay in place. There was a white SUV parked in the driveway. That was my brother's car, I thought to myself. And this was my brother's home.

"Do you want to go knock on the front door?" Cindy asked. Her tone was tentative. She was reading my mind. We hadn't planned to stop. But now . . .

I pictured myself walking up that driveway, past that car to the front door. I imagined knocking, hearing footsteps inside, and then the door opening.

Who would be standing there? Richard or his wife? How would I begin the conversation?

Hello. You're not going to believe this . . .

This was my moment—my opportunity to reach out and begin my journey with the Wyman family. We were here. We had come all this way. All I had to do was get out of the car and take that first step.

Turn the engine off.
Unlatch the seat belt.
Open the car door and go.
Just do it.
Now. Go!

I don't know how long we sat there. It wasn't long. Less than thirty seconds probably, but it felt longer. I had no sense of time, really. We just sat there and Cindy didn't say a word. This was my decision, and I had strong feelings both ways. Getting out of the car would be exciting. A new beginning. But I also might regret it. Were there things about this I hadn't thought of yet? Unintended consequences I couldn't have anticipated? What if the Wymans responded with anger and lashed out at my mother? They could make things ugly if they wanted to.

Slowly I took my foot off the brake and let the car begin to roll forward without taking my eyes off the house. I touched the gas pedal and felt the car lurch. I looked at Cindy. She had a sympathetic look on her face. Still no words.

I focused on the road ahead as we picked up speed. My secret would remain a secret for now, and I felt—what?—safe and protected. And maybe a little disappointed. I turned right at the end of the street and headed back to town in search of dinner.

On our final morning in Arizona we headed back to the cemetery. I pulled into the entrance and parked under a shade tree. It was 9:30 and the temperature was already in the upper eighties. It was going to be another very hot day.

We began our hunt for the graves of Gene and his wife, who had died several years before he did, by systematically moving from section to section and headstone to headstone, just as we had done countless times in other cemeteries on other ancestor hunts. But this cemetery was more modern than we were used to. These headstones were clean and polished and easy to read, and the grass framing them was a hearty Bermuda that thrived in hot, dry conditions.

At ten o'clock, after thirty minutes and no result, I walked to the office, which had just opened, and gave the woman behind the counter the name I was looking for. She looked it up in a large book and wrote down the section and row number on a piece of paper. By the time I got back outside, Cindy had already found it.

She pointed to it as I walked up. My father's headstone. It said "Eugene C. Wyman," and below it were the years of his birth and death. Almost immediately, without warning, my eyes began to well up. I was suddenly overwhelmed by more thoughts and feelings than I could handle. Gene Wyman and I had been on earth at the same time for more than forty years, but now he was gone. I was too late. I would never look him in the eye and take the measure of the man. Never shake his hand. Never hear his voice.

My cousin Nancy had dismissed him as nothing more than my sperm donor, which was true. But he could have been so much more. If circumstances had been different, I could have known my biological father. If my mother had put two and two together back in the day, or at least had had the courage to admit it, I might have grown up knowing both of my fathers.

But I knew I was fooling myself. In the mid-1950s, when I was born, such an outcome wouldn't have been allowed. There was no way my mother would have admitted such a thing, and no way my biological father would have cheerfully accepted me. There would have been shame and guilt all around, and unkind whispers in our neighborhood and at church and among family members.

No, I did not blame my mother for keeping it all a secret. But still, the headstone before me represented a road not taken, a missed opportunity, and a relationship that might have been, and I wept, thinking about all of it. It was all so sad. Gene Wyman and I were total strangers, and we always would be.

We took a few photographs of the grave, got back in our car, and I started the engine, but I couldn't drive yet. The world was a blur through my tears, so Cindy and I sat in the front seat a while longer, and without a word she took my hand as I sobbed, mourning a man I would never know.

CHAPTER 33

Father's Day

June 16, 2013

Father's Day arrived. It had been nine months since I had learned about my first DNA test result, and I was still searching for level ground. Some days were better than others, but there were times when my new reality was overwhelming and kept me in a state of anxiety. I rolled out of bed and checked my e-mail. The first message I opened was only four words long.

Thinking of you today.

It was from a TV executive in Los Angeles. She and her husband and Cindy and I had been friends for a long time. She was one of the few people to whom I had confided my secret.

Thinking of you today, she'd written. Not *Happy Father's Day.*

There was no doubt that this was going to be a confusing day emotionally. I would be a father and spend time with Chad and Carlee, and I would be a son and miss my own father and wish he were still around to celebrate with. And of course Charles Griffeth wasn't the only father I had to think about on this day. For the rest of my life there would always be two to remember.

It still did not seem right to call Gene Wyman my father, even though he was the one who gave me my Y chromosome—the very definition of a father. But that was all I shared with him, our DNA. We did not share memories. He did not teach me how to shoot a basket or ride a bicycle. Charles Griffeth did. One man gave me his genes and the other gave me his love.

But that kind of reasoning ignored the truth. Cousin Nancy, when she downplayed Gene's importance in my life with her "sperm donor" characterization, was only trying to help me work through the pain and confusion and make me feel better. But I was coming around to the notion that the best thing for me to do would be to stop sugarcoating my situation in euphemisms and see it for what it was. My complicated paternity was real and it wasn't going away. And my friend in Los Angeles knew that.

Thinking of you today.

I tried a mental exercise while I made my morning coffee, fantasizing about what I would have done with each of my fathers if they had been around on this Father's Day.

With Gene Wyman, we would start off by playing an early round of golf at his country club. I love desert golf, especially in the morning when the air is comfortably warm and dry and the shadows are long and the rising sun colors everything orange. I pictured us teeing off where Cindy and I had stood a week earlier, and then walking together down the fairway. My sense is Gene was an impatient, competitive man, and I imagine that was how he approached his golf game. He would expect to play quickly and would play to win, and compliments for good shots would be given only sparingly—all of which would inspire me to beat him without reservation.

After golf we would enjoy the club's Father's Day brunch. There would be rounds of Bloody Marys, omelets, roast beef, grilled tomatoes and asparagus, scalloped potatoes, and tempting desserts. We would spend the time reliving our morning round hole by hole, and laughing about the balls that ended up in the water or behind a cactus.

After brunch we would head home to watch the fourth and final round of the U.S. Open, the national championship of golf, which would be played later that afternoon. In 2013, pro golfer Phil Mickelson was the leader after the first three rounds. I was a big fan of Mickelson, in part because we both play golf left-handed, and I bet Gene would have been a fan too, because Phil played college golf in Arizona.

On my Father's Day with Charles Griffeth, we would begin our day at church. After my parents retired and bought their small farm in Tehachapi, they joined with other retirees in the area and actually started a United Methodist church. Initially they met each Sunday in the chapel of the local funeral parlor, a modest, non-denominational facility that the congregation eventually outgrew.

My folks were understandably proud of the faith community they had helped create, and they remained active in "their" church for several years.

After services, we would head home and Dad would barbecue homegrown steaks. During the seven years they lived on their farm, Mom and Dad raised a few head of cattle and kept the whole family supplied with fresh beef. We would eat our Father's Day lunch outside on the patio and enjoy the high desert breeze and the view of the Tehachapi Mountains.

Later that day Dad and I would watch basketball, game five of the NBA finals. On Father's Day in 2013 the Miami Heat and the San Antonio Spurs were tied at two games apiece, in a battle between two great teams and two great superstars, LeBron James versus Tim Duncan. Dad and I would root for the Spurs, since they represented our Western Conference.

Two fathers, two different Father's Days: one involving the comfortable life of privilege I had become accustomed to as an adult, and the other the down-home Midwestern simplicity I'd known as a child.

Here is what I actually did on that Father's Day: Cindy and Chad and Carlee and I went to church in the morning, we had a light snack for lunch, and then we spent the afternoon relaxing by our pool. Simple and satisfying.

I sat in a lounge chair and read the Sunday paper, enjoying the warm, sunny day. But my mind strayed and I thought some more about my two fathers. They'd had some things in common. Both grew up in Kansas. Both were star athletes in high school. And both were skilled woodworkers.

Had they ever met? Mom had worked for Wyman Construction for two years. In that time, Charles and Gene might have had an opportunity to come face to face. What would they have talked about? Dad was shy and reserved, and my sense of Gene was that he was a more outgoing, back-slapping kind of guy. So if they did meet, my guess is Gene would have done all the talking and Dad would have just listened and smiled and nodded his head. Dad took life as it came, but Gene had ambitions. Like me.

Dad was the bigger man. In his youth, he was tall and athletic, with muscular Popeye arms. As he aged, he slowed down and had to watch his weight. Gene had a sleeker physique that he was able to maintain throughout his life. Like me.

The other thing they had in common was Mom. In a way, for a time she ran both of their lives. There was no question that she was in charge of the Griffeth household, and at Wyman Construction her job was to supervise the office and make sure it all ran smoothly.

Charles and Gene also had one more thing in common. Me. The surprising little bundle of—was it joy? Was Dad suspicious when Mom suddenly became pregnant fifteen years after their last child was born? And did Gene even know he had fathered a child with Mom when she abruptly quit her job? She has never fully explained that.

Later in the afternoon when it was time to barbecue, I put on my denim apron, prepared the meat and vegetables, opened a bottle of wine, and we began our celebration. Cindy and the kids set the table by the pool, and we ate our Father's Day meal outside as the sun slipped toward the horizon. The whole time, the three of them kept exchanging furtive glances. They didn't think I noticed, but I did. Something was up.

After dinner Cindy said, "Do you want your present now?"

"Sure!" I said. But where was it? There was no wrapped package in view.

"Go get it," Cindy said to Chad and Carlee.

They disappeared around the side of the house and returned lugging a potted plant, which they placed on the deck in front of me. It was a palm tree, roughly two feet tall, probably the same height as the ones Gene had planted in front of the homes he'd built fifty years ago in Arizona.

I will probably never have a keepsake from Gene Wyman. Certainly nothing personal or that he made himself, like the small bookcase Dad built for me when I was in high school that I still cherish. This two-foot palm would have to do. It symbolized the personal touch he added to each of the homes his company built—his signature. And now it could be for me a remembrance of the father I would never know. The stranger in my genes.

I looked at Cindy.

"Happy Father's Day," she said with a mischievous grin.

CHAPTER 34

New Ancestor Hunt

October 20, 2014

"Are you a Wyman?" The woman's voice on my cell phone was cheerful and friendly. Her accent betrayed only the slightest hint of the South.

I paused, unsure how to answer.

Cindy and I were sitting in our car in the parking lot of a Methodist church in Tennessee.

A rainstorm had come and gone, and beads of water clung to the windshield, blurring our view of the small country cemetery in front of us. A cemetery where many of the headstones said "Wyman."

It was the fall of 2014. Two years had passed since the impact of my initial DNA test had sent me reeling into months of disbelief and anguish. The shock had slowly receded and, little by little—day by day—time was healing the wounds. I was beginning to accept this bizarre turn of events in my life. Although many questions remained, because my mother and I no longer talked about my DNA issue, I knew they would likely never be answered. I was going to have to learn to live with them. At this point curiosity had replaced distress, and I was ready to embrace the hunt for my alternate-universe family history. And so we had driven to Tennessee.

Family histories are like religious creation stories. They can give meaning to our lives. There is a logical progression to the generations in a family that emerges when their saga is examined years after the fact. And the ancestral stories we pass down, or discover, are the legends that define us. They can be inspiring, instructive, sometimes distressing, and sometimes even comforting.

Tennessee was where my earliest known Wyman ancestors, my fourth great-grandparents Jonathan and Rosemary Wyman, settled in the 1780s and where my third great-grandfather, Thomas, was born. The Wymans had come to Tennessee from somewhere in the

Northeast. It is unclear why they migrated when they did and why they chose Tennessee, but they did, and Tennessee is where most of Jonathan and Rosemary's descendants remain to this day. I wanted to see this place where my roots—my new roots—extended.

We crossed into eastern Tennessee from North Carolina, heading west along Route 40, and climbed into the Great Smoky Mountains. The fall colors were at their peak, and they were magnificent. The crimsons and golds had an intensity that I'd thought existed only in New England.

The Wymans initially lived along the banks of the Nolichucky River. The terrain reminded us of parts of Virginia and the Carolinas that were familiar to us, with their thick pine forests and wide, muddy rivers. We drove the tree-lined road that hugged the river's winding southern bank for several miles. In her research, Cindy had identified the place where the Wymans had lived, and we stopped there and got out of our car to explore. The sun was shining brightly and the air was crisp and cool.

I walked along the river with the odd name and tried to feel the presence of the people who made up the history of the Wyman family, just as I had felt the presence of my Griffeth ancestors when I walked the beaches of Cape Cod or the cornfields of Illinois. But here I felt nothing. Truthfully, while I now accepted my Wyman heritage, I had not yet embraced it. Intellectually I understood that Gene Wyman's Y chromosome was also in me, but emotionally I felt no primal stirring, no familial connection. It was going to take more time.

We got back in our car and left the Smoky Mountains for the flatlands of central Tennessee where the Wymans had eventually settled for good. After a while I turned off the main highway and drove on muddy country roads so we could get a close-up view of the fields of tobacco that extended for miles in all directions. The Griffeth farms I knew in Kansas had grown wheat and corn. But in Tennessee, tobacco was the commodity that had sustained the lives of the Wymans. Early Native Americans had for centuries smoked it in pipes for medicinal purposes. When they introduced it to English colonists in the 1600s it quickly became a popular cash crop that the colonists shipped back to European markets.

I had never seen tobacco plants in person. The type grown in this part of Tennessee, called Burley, is commonly used in cigarettes. Almost all of the fields had recently been harvested, and the tobacco leaves, which reminded me of giant collard greens, were hanging in clusters to dry in open-air barns and shacks. There, they would gradually change color from green to gold and finally to the familiar shade of tobacco brown.

This was the land where Jonathan and Rosemary Wyman raised their nine children. After they died in the early 1800s, all but one of their children remained in Tennessee. Only my ancestor, Thomas, moved on. He migrated west, and eventually his descendants ended up in Kansas. The rest of the Wyman family lived in and around a town located several miles from the Nolichucky. Four generations lived there, spanning almost two hundred years. They were farmers and merchants and preachers. They were also slave owners. Before our trip, Cindy and I had found slave inventories in online census records for the Wymans, and wills that bequeathed human property from one generation to the next. Not surprisingly, the Civil War soldiers in the family fought for the Confederacy. In a sense, they took up arms against my Griffeth ancestors, who fought for the Union.

Tobacco and slaves and Confederate soldiers. All part of my new heritage and identity. And all very unnerving.

After a couple of hours on the road, we came to the town where my distant Wyman cousins lived, just as a cluster of storm clouds rolled in. We drove down the main street and zigzagged past the modest homes. There was an energy to the area that I liked very much. Most of the towns where my Griffeth ancestors lived in Kansas and Nebraska had been virtually abandoned during the demise of the farm economy in the 1960s and '70s. But here in this Tennessee town there was life—a future. Raindrops began to fall as we passed under homemade banners hanging over several streets, all of them supporting the local high school football team. And we saw subtle evidence of the Wyman family's presence, including a Wyman Street and a storefront sign for the Wyman Insurance Agency. But we were not there to meet these people. We wanted only to acquaint ourselves with their ancestors.

So we headed to the cemetery on the western edge of town, across the street from the local Methodist church.

It was a typical old country graveyard. The citizens of the town had been burying their dead there since the mid-1800s. Between rain showers Cindy and I slogged through the mud and wet grass and studied each Wyman headstone, slowly taking note of the names in my extended family tree. The earliest moss-covered gravestones were worn down by the elements, making their inscriptions difficult to read. We had done this countless times in other cemeteries all over the country as we'd researched both of our families' histories, so we had the routine down pat. Cindy wrote down names and dates in a small note pad while I took photographs, and we paused at each headstone to figure out the family connections.

The oldest grave in the yard belonged to Jeremiah Wyman, a younger brother of my ancestor Thomas and the patriarch of the many Wymans who lived in the area. From what we had learned, Jeremiah's life read like a Faulkner novel. He was a wealthy gentleman farmer who owned a thousand-acre tobacco plantation and more than a dozen slaves. He and his wife, Sarah, who was also his first cousin, had eleven children, some of whom also married Wyman cousins. Jeremiah was a respected member of the community until he met a sudden and dramatic end when he was dragged to death by a team of runaway horses. Sarah's grave was next to his; she outlived him by more than thirty years. All around them were a dozen or so headstones for their children, grandchildren, and great-grandchildren.

When we finished our task we walked across the road to the church, to see if someone there could tell us anything more about the Wymans buried in the cemetery. The sanctuary was a sturdy red brick building. The wooden cross atop the tall white steeple stood out against the black clouds in the sky.

We opened the office door just as the church secretary was hanging up the phone. There were two people ahead of us waiting to talk to her, but when she spotted us, the strangers, she immediately gave us her full attention. I started to explain our interest in the Wyman family.

She interrupted me: "You just missed the annual Wyman family reunion!" It turned out that dozens of cousins from around the region and from different states had gathered at the church only two days earlier for a potluck supper. "And they were selling a book about the Wyman family history," she added.

"Do you have any copies?" I asked.

"No, but let me give you the phone number of the woman who does." She scribbled a name and number on a Post-it note and handed it to me. We thanked her and headed out to the parking lot just as a new rain shower was passing through.

"Are you going to call her?" Cindy asked as we got into our car.

I studied the piece of paper. My heart rate picked up and the rain outside got heavier. The noisy patter on the car roof unsettled me. I had experienced many pivotal moments in the previous two years. Moments when I had to make important decisions. *Should I take a second DNA test? Should I ask my mother who my father was? Should I reach out to my half siblings?*

This one didn't feel as weighty, I told myself. It was a simple phone call. I only wanted to buy a book—no big deal. So why was my heart racing? I punched in the numbers on my cell phone and held my breath.

"Hello?" The woman who answered was clearly elderly. Her voice trembled, and she spoke slowly and deliberately. I identified myself, explained how I had gotten her number, and asked about the book on the Wyman family history.

"Yes," she said, "we still have copies. How many would you like?" The congenial tone of her voice calmed me. I gave her my name and address, and she told me where to mail my check.

Then came the question I hadn't expected: "Are you a Wyman?" She was just being neighborly, making casual conversation. She had no way of knowing the great anxiety her question was causing. The rain had suddenly stopped, and I could see the headstones off in the distance through the wet windshield.

Here it was again: another moment. Another decision. I looked at Cindy, who was smiling her reassuring smile.

"Yes," I said as I stared into Cindy's eyes. "As a matter of fact, I am a Wyman."

Epilogue

May 2016

Almost four years after the initial shock of my first DNA test and the many surprising revelations and discoveries that followed, I thought nothing else about this story could surprise me. And then this happened.

One evening in the spring of 2016, just as we were putting the finishing touches on this book, I came home from work and Cindy greeted me with a mischievous grin.

"I have something to show you," she said as she handed me a small greeting card.

The illustration on the front was of an infant lying in a giant baby bootie decorated with red roses and blue ribbons. The card was clearly old. The colors had faded almost to a pastel. In old-fashioned script, the headline at the top read: "Congratulations Mother and Dad."

"What's this?" I asked.

"I found it today while I was going through a box your mother sent us years ago," Cindy said. "It was with several other congratulatory cards your parents received when you were born. Open it." Inside there was a poem:

Everyone loves a baby,
So precious, so small, so new!
Dear mother and dad,
We're ever so glad
Such a dear one has come to you

At the bottom, in a carefully handwritten script, was this:

Is it too early?
Gene

I gasped. Cindy laughed.

"You have *got* to be kidding," I said. I examined the card more closely, turning it over and over, as its significance sunk in. Several things occurred to me all at once, and I tried to sort them out.

If this card was indeed from Gene Wyman—who else could it have been?—then it meant he had known I exist. He had to have known that Mom was pregnant when she quit her job at Wyman Construction, and I have to believe that he at least considered the possibility that the child was his.

I studied the handwriting. He had signed his name with an upward slant, and he underlined it as if to add a flourish. Just what I would have expected from the self-assured businessman I believe he was.

This card is now the most tangible connection I have to my biological father. I had toured the town where he lived, the club where he played golf, and the cemetery where he was buried, all in an effort to establish a bond with his memory. But he had actually held this card in his hands, just as I was doing. And he had signed it while thinking of my mother, and of the child he may have suspected was his. Me. This gave me the connection I had been seeking.

But what did he mean by "Is it too early?" He didn't write "Congratulations!" or "Very happy for you!" He wrote "Is it too early?" I could speculate all day about what he meant, but ultimately I'll never know. And it doesn't really matter. I'm going to have the baby card framed and put it in my office next to the photo I have of Gene Wyman, and near a photo of Mom and Dad. When I look at all of it, I will think of family.

What brought my mother and Gene Wyman together will probably remain a mystery to me. Given his early marriage history, it would be easy to dismiss him as a cad and a philanderer. But I choose not to be too judgmental—after all, I didn't know the man. And I am not inclined to make excuses for my mother, either. I was shocked by what she did because I had placed her on a pedestal. I truly believed that she could do no wrong. But I realize now that by idolizing her the way I did, I didn't allow myself to see the complete woman. It turned out she was just like everyone else, a good person capable of sinful thoughts and actions.

I am often asked whether I will ever reach out to the Wyman family. The short answer is no, but I can never say never. Would I like to see more photos of Gene Wyman and hear stories about his life? Of course I would, but would it be worth the cost? It would mean disrupting the lives of his children and grandchildren and forever altering their view of him, and they don't deserve that. If Gene Wyman were still alive, I would definitely contact him. But he's not. Thank goodness for the Internet. It has helped me find answers to many of my questions about the Wyman family's history and provided me with the broad outline of my biological father's life. For now, at least, that's enough for me.

Another question that comes up frequently is: What is my relationship with my mother like? In many ways, nothing has changed. When I phone her, we talk about the weather and she tells me about events at her assisted-living complex, and I tell her about what Chad and Carlee are up to. When we get together, we look at old family photos, and she reminisces about her childhood. But some things are not the same. My DNA issue hovers over us but neither of us ever acknowledges it. If my mother were willing to talk about it, I would listen with great interest. But she's not, and I'm not willing to press her to reveal her deepest secrets just to satisfy my curiosity. Unless my mother decides to talk, those secrets will remain locked in her heart, and she will take them with her when she passes on. And I'm OK with that.

After all the gut-wrenching angst and life-altering drama that resulted from that initial DNA test, I can say without reservation that I am at peace. As devastated as I was to discover the truth about the circumstances of my birth, I am also eternally grateful.

In case you're wondering, Mom gave her approval to this book. Even though she doesn't like to talk about it, she understands my need to tell this story. Her only request was that I never change my name to Wyman. I smiled and promised her that I would always be a Griffeth.

Acknowledgments

This book went through many, many revisions as it morphed from personal journal into finished product. I thank those of my friends who were kind enough to read the earliest and roughest drafts. They include my literary hero, author Lawrence Goldstone, who read the very first draft and—as usual—offered valuable constructive criticism; former newspaper editor Lou Golden, a longtime friend who provided wise counsel over long dinners that went late into the evening; prolific author and editor Christopher John Farley, who "got" this book right away and gave me such great feedback; CNBC's biotech correspondent Meg Tirrell, who helped me understand the science of DNA (if any mistakes still exist in the book, trust me, they are all mine); my former producer Alison Singer, who was such a strong advocate for my mother's side of the story; and my college pal Dr. Lori Baker-Schena, who challenged me when I needed to be challenged.

Heartfelt thanks also to go to my friend and agent Larry Kramer, who expertly shepherded this project through every stage; to literary agent Claudia Cross, who was an early champion of this book; to my very patient attorney James Gregorio; to my boss Nik Deogun, CNBC senior vice president and editor-in-chief, who was fascinated by my story from day one; and to CNBC president Mark Hoffman, another Valley boy who made good, and who has long been my supporter, for which I am grateful.

And then there are the wonderful folks at the New England Historic Genealogical Society. First and foremost, thanks go to my dear friend, the Society's President and CEO, Brenton Simons, who generously offered to publish this book even before one word was written; to COO Ryan Woods, who was instrumental in making this book a reality; and to my beloved editors: Publishing Director Penelope Stratton and Lynn Betlock, managing editor of *American Ancestors* magazine. They asked all the right questions, saw things

I didn't see, and helped me find the true meaning of this book. Thanks also to the Society's Director of Marketing and Sales, Jim Power, for his great enthusiasm and many ideas; to Publications Coordinator Ellen Maxwell for the perfect cover design; and to copyeditor Julie Hagen who so tactfully corrected my many excesses and errors and made it a better book in the process.

Thanks also to my close friends Tim and Janet Shine and Karin and Leo Nemetz, who lived through all of this craziness with me and helped me maintain my sanity with their humor and encouragement. And to the members of my wife's book club who read an early draft and spent an evening grilling me with important, thought-provoking questions.

And there is my family: My children Chad and Carlee, whose resilience through this turbulent time helped me keep my perspective; my big brother, Chuck, and my sister-in-law, Terryll, who were willing to take this journey with me (and I'm thankful they did); Cousin Nancy who was like a guardian angel resting on my shoulder whispering her words of encouragement; and, of course, my wonderfully meddlesome cousin Doug, who has been the voice of reason from day one.

What can I say about my wife, Cindy? She held me together with her love and never gave up on me. I love you to infinity and beyond.

Finally: Thank you, Mom. I owe you my life.

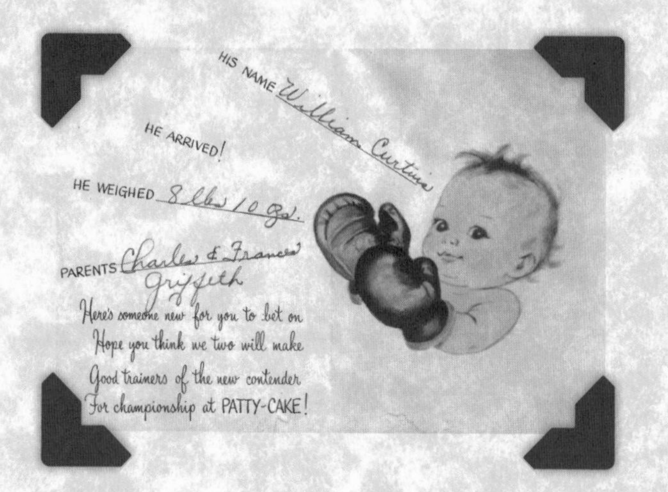
HIS NAME William Curtis
HE ARRIVED!
HE WEIGHED 8 lbs 10 ozs.
PARENTS Charles & Frances Griffith
Here's someone new for you to bet on
Hope you think we two will make
Good trainers of the new contender
For championship at PATTY-CAKE!